MARIENTHAL

MARIENTHAL

The Sociography of an Unemployed Community

Marie Jahoda, Paul F. Lazarsfeld, and Hans Zeisel

With a new introduction by **Christian Fleck**

Transaction Publishers
New Brunswick (U.S.A.) and London (U.K.)

Fourth printing 2009

New material this edition copyright © 2002 by Transaction Publishers, New Brunswick, New Jersey. Originally published in 1971 by Transaction Publishers.

All rights reserved under International and Pan-American Copyright Conventions. No part of this book may be reproduced or transmitted in any form or by any means, electronic or mechanical, including photocopy, recording, or any information storage and retrieval system, without prior permission in writing from the publisher. All inquiries should be addressed to AldineTransaction, A Division of Transaction Publishers, Rutgers—The State University of New Jersey, 35 Berrue Circle, Piscataway, New Jersey 08854-8042. www.transactionpub.com

This book is printed on acid-free paper that meets the American National Standard for Permanence of Paper for Printed Library Materials.

Library of Congress Catalog Number: 2002028627
ISBN: 978-0-7658-0944-5
Printed in the United States of America

Library of Congress Cataloging-in-Publication Data

Jahoda, Marie.
   [Arbeitslosen von Marienthal, English]
  Marienthal : the sociography of an unemployed community / Marie Jahoda, Paul F. Lazarsfeld, and Hans Zeisel ; with a new introduction by Christian Fleck.
     p. cm.
  Originally published: Chicago : Aldine, 1971.
  Includes bibliographical references and index.
  ISBN 0-7658-0944-3 (alk. paper)
    1. Unemployed—Austria—Marienthal. 2. Social surveys—History.
 I. Lazarsfeld, Paul Felix. II. Zeisel, Hans. III. Title.

HD5772.M33 J3   2002
305.9'06941043615—dc21   2002028627

Contents

INTRODUCTION TO THE TRANSACTION EDITION	vii
FOREWORD TO THE AMERICAN EDITION	
Forty Years Later	xxxi
1. Introduction	1
2. The Industrial Village	11
3. The Living Standard	17
4. Menus and Budgets	25
5. A Weary Community	36
6. Response to Deprivation	45
7. The Meaning of Time	66
8. Fading Resilience	78
AFTERWORD	
Toward a History of Sociography	99
Index	127

Introduction to the Transaction Edition

RARELY DOES a sociological study become a movie script. Even more rarely does this happen some fifty years after the book's first edition came out. When in 1988 Marie Jahoda, one of the surviving authors from the group which originally conducted *Marienthal*, saw the semi-documentary television drama, directed by the late Karin Brandauer, an experienced Austrian film director, she was astonished by what a filmmaker could make out of a social research study. Despite Jahoda's objections to the sentimental mood and some misinterpretations, this film has gained the status of introductory material for university courses in sociology and psychology in Germany and Austria ever since. The film's title cites a line from one of the time sheets an unemployed man from Marienthal village filled out around the turn of the year 1931 to 1932: *Einstweilen wird es Mittag* (In the meantime, midday comes around). Using time sheets was only one of the inventions elaborated in this exemplary study, and quoting ordinary people at some length occurred only seldom in scholarly publications at this time in Central Europe. The story of this innovative investigation, the fate of its authors and the book itself provide instructive insights into the history of European social research of the 1930s and beyond.

vii

viii   *Introduction to the Transaction Edition*

The Book

The original title of the small book is both telling and strange: *Die Arbeitslosen von Marienthal, ein soziographischer Versuch über die Wirkungen langdauernder Arbeitslosigkeit, mit einem Anhang zur Geschichte der Soziographie, bearbeitet und herausgegeben von der Österreichischen Wirtschaftspsychologischen Forschungsstelle* ("The Unemployed of Marienthal: A Sociographic Essay on the Consequences of Long-Term Unemployment, with an Appendix on the History of Sociography, treated and edited by the Austrian Research Unit for Economic Psychology.") In reading the baroque-sounding title, one could, however, grasp the manifest meaning of the book's content. A study about the consequences of being unemployed, but from which point of view, by using what approach, from what branch of the social sciences, and by whom?

Eight chapters running over some eighty printed pages, not a single reference to the scientific literature in the main body of the book, some simple tables, no real statistical analysis. On the other hand the authors used a vivid, down-to-earth language to give the reader a detailed portrait of the everyday life of an unemployed community during what in Europe was then called the Worldwide Economic Crisis and became know in the United States as the Great Depression.

An American browsing through the shelves of a university library or bookstore who opens this small book might be reminded of studies by students of the Chicago sociologist Robert E. Park. Even readers with more than a slight familiarity with the history of the social sciences in Europe seldom would detect that this piece stems from German authors. Nevertheless the so-called Chicago School did not have any direct influence on the group of researchers in interwar Vienna nor were they influenced by German social scientists of their time.

Only the introduction to *Marienthal* accommodates to conventional scholarly routines by informing the reader about what the researchers were reaching for and what they had actually done. Available statistics are superficial and reports by journalists cover only exemplary cases, claim the authors in the first paragraph. They had wanted to bridge the gap between those two approaches and

Introduction to the Transaction Edition ix

had tried to elude accidental impressions. The proposed "comprehensive picture of life in Marienthal" (2) is delivered through the rest of the book.

A tiny community some twenty miles southeast of Austria's capital, Vienna, Marienthal was created as an offspring of a flax mill in the first third of the nineteenth century. Around the mill, later enlarged to a factory, hired laborers from different corners of the Hapsburg Empire had settled and had become permanent inhabitants during the next hundred years. After the collapse of the monarchy at the end of World War I, the labor movement became stronger and used its influence to go on strike in the early 1920s. Only a few months later, a first wave of layoffs started, but the factory recovered and was in full workload until the Austrian bank system collapsed in the spring of 1929, sweeping along all those corporations reliant on the availability of bank loans. Over the summer of 1929 the factory and all its companion plants closed down and nearly every family in the small village became affected by unemployment. The big difference from former recessions was the sheer length of time this unemployment lasted. When the researchers first came to Marienthal more than two years after the shutdown of the factory, the situation had not changed at all; it had became even worse.

Chapter 3 on the "Living Standard" provides details about the living conditions in Marienthal. Only one out of five families had at least one member earning an income from regular work. Three-quarters of the families were dependent on unemployment payments, which were dramatically low at this time. From those individuals on relief only the tiny minority of 5 percent received the then maximum of sixty shillings (or $ 102 in 2000 prices) per month and "consumer unit" (for the definition of consumer unit see note 2 on page 20). Here, and elsewhere, the study does not pause by giving raw data about income and usage of it but turns immediately to the experiences of the hungry people. So called "family protocols" present vivid descriptions of the struggle for survival in this desperate community. Allotments were the only legal remedies, but "when a dog disappears, the owner no longer bothers to report the loss" (22).

Contrary to the then well-established routines of social bookkeeping developed by members of the *Verein für Socialpolitik x*   *Introduction to the Transaction Edition*

(Association for Social Policy)[1] and social reportages used by the labor movement press the investigators moved on. The second half of the study is devoted entirely to the socio-psychological consequences of unemployment.

Starting with a portrait of "A Weary Community" the authors demonstrate the far-reaching consequences of the situation. Before the recession took place, Marienthal was a stronghold of the Social Democratic Labor Movement. There was a full-fledged Workers' Library, newspapers were widely distributed and read, participation in the community's life was strong, many clubs were active and participation in political campaigns and elections was high. Nearly everything had come to a stop after the closing of the factory and the following catastrophe. People who should have more time for reading books stopped borrowing them from the library; newspapers were not read as carefully as before, if at all; only organizations offering their members direct financial advantages showed an increase, in particular the Social Democratic cremation society and the cycling club, because of the insurance it provided to its membership.

Furthermore there were "Responses to Deprivation," as the title of chapter 6 indicates. Here the reader finds what the German original specified more precisely as *Die Haltung* (meaning stance or attitude in a non-technical sense). A typology based on a close examination of some hundred families found four different *Haltungen* (attitudes): "unbroken – resigned – in despair – apathetic." Moreover the authors made a cross-tabulation between their psychologically grounded classifications and the average income per consumer unit (again, they did not call it this way, as they did not make use of the sociological or psychological concept "attitude" in the German original). The lower the income the more deprived the families reacted. Someone whose earnings were as low as thirty-four shillings a month (or $ 58 at 2000 prices) counts still as unbroken, whereas families with a monthly income between nineteen to twenty-five shillings (or $ 32 to $ 42) fall in the category of broken (combining the two lowest levels of adaptation). These findings have become common knowledge for social scientists in the meantime and were confirmed more than once, but were a surprise in 1933. Political activists and social scientists expected

Introduction to the Transaction Edition   *xi*

a more active, rebellious reaction to deprivation then; Marxists of all branches anticipated the revolution to come after the final breakdown of capitalism. *Marienthal* provided a telling lesson quite contrary to the conventional wisdom and history itself validated the experience.

A particularly interesting part of the study is chapter 7 on "The Meaning of Time." The insights presented there truly "emerged as a temporary derivative rather than as a focus for a continuing research program," as Robert K. Merton noted in his seminal paper on Socially Expected Durations.[2] The observations which led to the findings were neither part of the initial planning of the research team nor were they embedded in contemporary research styles or theories. A sociology of time was then still unknown. What the researchers figured out in Marienthal about the usage of time was completely unexpected but nevertheless important for further research. It was serendipitous. Near the very end of their stay in Marienthal, someone from the research group called attention to the fact that men walked more slowly across the main street and stopped more often on their way than women. Immediately they turned their attention to this behavior, they fetched a stopwatch and started to count the number of times people stopped and measured the walking speed from a concealed position. A conclusion of their unobtrusive observations was that women were not really unemployed but only unpaid: "They have the household to run, which fully occupies the day" (74). Not only did the researchers discover something unexpected about time use but also about gender differences in coping with unemployment. Both insights resulted from carefully conducted observations and as a result of an unprejudiced interpretation of empirical data.

The concluding chapter raises the question "How long can this life continue?" The authors did not feel in a position to give a sound answer as they frankly indicated. However, they draw the reader's attention to another point of view, the biographical dimension of coping with unfortunate conditions of life. Those people who "had been particularly well-off in the past were apt to develop a different reaction to unemployment" (94). Lack of resources prevented the researchers to elaborate this point further. The main text closes with a telling sentence: "We entered Marienthal as scien-

xii *Introduction to the Transaction Edition*

tists; we leave it with only one desire: that the tragic opportunity for such an inquiry may not recur in our time" (98).

Consequently the authors did not lose their interest in the fate of the people of Marienthal after they had finished their investigation and published their findings. Late in 1933, Marie Jahoda returned to Marienthal to see what had happened there since the team finished its investigation: "During the whole time of our investigation in Marienthal the desire sprouted in every member of the research group for once not to be restricted to the role of the investigator who describes but to organize and to help." In a memo to Paul Lazarsfeld who lived in New York at this time Jahoda summarized her experiences and discussed one major obstacle at some length. The new authoritarian regime had established its own scheme to give work to the unemployed by forcing them to join the Freiwilliger Arbeitsdienst (Voluntary Work Service). Despite her strong opposition to nearly everything which stemmed from the "dictatorship mitigated by sloppiness," as the regime of Engelbert Dollfuss and his successor Kurt Schuschnigg was called by its Austrian opponents, Jahoda argued in favor of this welfare-to-work project: "Only the provision of any work could counter the resignation that comes with unemployment."[3]

The Methodology

The book's title refers to sociography as its methodology. Not only does this term sound unfamiliar today, it was so then as well. Why did the group around the young Paul Lazarsfeld not follow established paths, why did they feel encouraged to map out a new one? What was really new, and what was just a kind of re-invention? How did this innovation emerge, and why?

To answer these questions we can find some hints in the text itself because the authors report their research strategy at some length, although they neither compared their own way with those of competitors nor legitimized their decisions through discussing rival methodological options.

The research group did not waste its time debating preparatory meta-theoretical problems. Retracing their endeavor into the history of the social sciences is reserved for the appendix on the history of sociography, that was written after the investigation was

Introduction to the Transaction Edition   *xiii*

finished; the researchers started their project off the cuff. Preparations started in the autumn of 1931, with field-work beginning towards the end of the year when the young psychology graduate Lotte Danzinger went to Marienthal to live in the community for six weeks. "[C]ontact with the population was facilitated by Dr. Lotte Danziger's [sic!] preparatory work ...; she inspired the confidence to which we owe the copious biographical material" (6). Lotte Schenk-Danzinger, as she was called after her marriage, described her somewhat mixed feelings about her experiences in an interview conducted half a century later:

> "Well, I lived there for a while and did a number of interviews, but I really hated it. ... I had a terrible, an awful room, really awful. That was for about a week, or perhaps ten days .... I left the house in the morning and did a few interviews with different families, and then wrote them down in the afternoon, ... you could not really write them down in the presence of the people because then they would have immediately stopped telling their stories, so you had to draw up the protocols from memory."[4]

The fact that someone from outside the core group was commissioned to carry out the field-work most likely had very trivial reasons. Marie Jahoda was at the time completing her Ph.D. thesis and was studying for the final exams, Lazarsfeld was busy directing other surveys so that it was impossible for him to leave his workplace for any long period of time, and Hans Zeisel was working in his father's law office in Vienna, and was likewise unable to take an extended period of leave. We do not know how many temporary employees helped out occasionally, only that "ten psychologists" conducted the field-work and spent "some 120 working days" (9) there, Lotte Danzinger thus undertook about one-third of the overall workload in the field.[5]

That the three authors of *Marienthal*, who later became associated solely with the study, were only marginally involved in the field-work was balanced through meetings which were held once or twice a week and where "arrangements for the following days" (9) were made. This is worth mentioning because it underscores that no definite research design had been worked out in advance, but many possible techniques and approaches were discovered only in the course of the investigations. Therefore one major advantage of the study is that the team was flexible and did not insist *xiv*   *Introduction to the Transaction Edition*

on rigid methodological routines – they modified guidelines for the field-workers regularly.

Furthermore, it is worth mentioning that the senior researchers' lack of involvement in the process of data collection was not the consequence of a developed division of labor between different statuses inside the research team, where the researchers responsible for the design used unbiased field-workers for methodological reasons as became a common standard later on.

To identify the innovative character of *Marienthal* we have to use comparisons. Which of the techniques employed by the research team had been used before (in their own investigations or in studies by others), and, secondly, in which category would they fit according to our present classifications? As table 1 illustrates, the method most frequently employed today, that is, personal interviews in which subjects are asked about their views and attitudes, was of little significance then. If interviews were carried out at all, they followed very different guidelines from those used today. No questionnaire was utilized by the collaborators during their conversations with the villagers. Apart from official statistical information the researchers developed highly original methods of data collection which they had not encountered before, neither in their training nor in the relevant literature. The methods they could have been familiar with, from the surveys carried out by the *Verein für Socialpolitik* and from what they learned at the Department of Psychology at the University of Vienna, were experts interviews, the recording of life-histories, prompting of school essays and the use of psychological tests (shortage of funds restricted the scope of this technique, however).

In today's terminology one would classify the main method as "action research," although strictly speaking this is incorrect because the Marienthal team did not primarily seek to activate the respondents politically. Action research ultimately implies that the researchers know what is "good" for the community they investigate. Therefore research is interventionist, with the investigators seeking to generate the kind of social movement that they feel the community lacks. What distinguished the researchers in Marienthal was that they subordinated their objectives to the people's "needs." "We made it a consistent point of policy that none of our research-

Introduction to the Transaction Edition   xv

Table 1
Methods Used in Marienthal and Their Present-Day Counterparts

	Present day classification		Original notation
Unobtrusive data collection	Quantitative data	Official existing statistics	* Election results
			* Population statistics
			* Housekeeping Statistics
			* *Reports and complaints made to the Industrial Commission*
		Content analysis	* Account books
			* Library records (loans)
			* Subscriptions to newspapers
			* Membership figures of clubs
	Qualitative data		* Family Diaries
	Quantitative data	Structured observation	Measurement of walking speed
	Qualitative data	Participant observation	* *Visits to families*
		Action research	Clothing project
			Medical consultation
			Pattern design course
			Girls' gymnastics course
			Political activities
			* Parent Guidance
		Expert reports	* Reports from teachers, parish priest, town mayor, doctors, business people, officials from political clubs and other organizations
		Projective material	* School essays, prize essay competition
		Psychological tests	* Psychological tests
Intrusive data collection		Written records	Family files, with separate files for each member
	Quantitative data		* Meal records
	Quantitative data		Time sheets
	Qualitative data	Personal interviews	* Life Histories

Note: Asterisks in the right column indicate previous use in social science research projects.

ers should be in Marienthal as a mere reporter or outside observer. Everyone was to fit naturally into the communal life by participating in some activity generally useful to the community" (5).

Table 1 also clearly shows the "mixture of methods." The researchers used *triangulation* long before this kind of research was coined by Norman K. Denzin.[6] Efforts were made to employ different ways of collecting data or combinations of them. In an exemplary manner, *Marienthal* adhered to the principle that the methodology should be appropriate to the subject, and that the choice of methods should be appropriate to the circumstances.

Jahoda later recalled that "the methods emerged as a result of the concentration on the problem, and not for their own sake."[7]

xvi   *Introduction to the Transaction Edition*

Even before *Marienthal* was published, Zeisel presented similar arguments to counter any "criticism of our procedure." He rejects suggestions that the design they had selected displayed "little uniformity from the point of view of any specialized science" and did not respect the "methodological barriers, laboriously erected to keep psychology and sociology apart," by emphasizing "the special advantage" of the chosen approach, which according to Zeisel was that

> our design ... did not want to adopt a single uniform perspective, but allowed us to give a unified description of the social phenomenon which the unemployed village of Marienthal represented. The methodological advantage of this approach is directly linked to the ultimately applied purpose of social science research: It wants to provide a basis for our actions.[8]

This cursory glance at the methodology raises the question of what made this innovative approach possible. Again, because "about sixty-six pounds" (9) of the original materials were lost due to political circumstances, we have to try to reconstruct the answer from the surviving information. Lazarsfeld provides some clues as to what a possible answer might be in his introduction, where he discusses the problem of collecting the data:

> "Our idea was to find procedures which would combine the use of numerical data with immersion *(sich einleben)* into the situation. To this end it was necessary to gain such close contact with the population in Marienthal that we could learn the smallest details of their daily life. At the same time we had to perceive each day so that it was possible to reconstruct it objectively; finally, a structure had to be developed for the whole that would allow all the details to be seen as expressions of a minimum number of basic syndromes" (1f.).

Following the same line of argument, Zeisel emphasizes the importance of the American method of "unobtrusive observation" in those parts of the original appendix which were omitted from the American translation.[9] Contemporary readers of the study consequently felt that the greatest achievement of *Marienthal* was its "functional penetration," as O. A. Oeser called it:

> [T]he observers approach the community to be studied not as reporters with notebook and camera, but as far as possible as accepted members of

Introduction to the Transaction Edition   *xvii*

that community, having several definite and easily intelligible functions within it. It is clear that the frame of mind with which questions will be answered by a member of a community will depend on his attitude of acceptance, rejection, or neutrality towards the questioner. On the other hand, the fact that an observer has a part to play in a community makes it not only easier for him to ask questions, but will suggest many observations and questions that might otherwise not have occurred to him.[10]

Participation in activities helpful to members of the community, however, only becomes possible if several preconditions are met. First, the researcher will have to oppose the coercion towards ever-more rigid demarcation lines between the disciplines in their work, and then they will have to be prepared to abandon their socially elevated and secure position and relinquish the role of objective observing scholar, for reasons of *methodology*. This does not mean that they will have to regress to a dedicated attitude in which their personal involvement in the everyday life of the community overwhelms their role as observers. In fact, the approach might best be described by the following, almost paradoxical, characterization: The researchers temporarily join the social group they want to study. Acting the role of a new member of the group allows one to explain one's presence to the members of the community, as well as to find a more detached role within the community in which one will be able to pursue one's scholarly interests. Constantly one has to balance one role against the other, yet the "immersion into the situation" gives one "first-hand information and compassionate understanding"[11] of the social life one is investigating. Once the field-work has been completed, this knowledge will help the participant observer to arrive at a more valid interpretation and description of the social realities. It is only when the collected material is being *assessed* that quantification can start.

The usage of participant observation, unfamiliar in European social science circles of the time, was possible only because the researchers had distanced themselves from the contemporary European practice where social scientists were primarily concerned with achieving a maximum of objectivity, for reasons of reputation and as a consequence of their social status. Zeisel described this detachment in an article published simultaneously with *Marienthal*:

xviii   *Introduction to the Transaction Edition*

> Between the general overview which the statistical data of the contemporary administration network can give and the relatively abstract knowledge which science-based sociology provides there is a gap in our knowledge of social events. We feel that it should be the task of sociographic methods to fill this gap.[12]

Another factor, supporting the innovative character of the study, was the positive reception of behaviorism by the Bühler School, where the new ideas were never allowed to ossify into sterile dogma, but inspired a certain methodological approach. Lazarsfeld's comment that the team tried "to illustrate the psychological aspect of unemployment using modern research methods" was therefore a very apt description of their objectives.[13] In addition, the *Forschungsstelle* received through the intercession of the Bühlers' money from the Rockefeller Foundation to realize the proposed study of an unemployed community (additional small funds came from the Viennese Chamber of Labor, under its Social Democratic leadership).

Listing only the cognitive aspects which made *Marienthal* an innovative study would create an incomplete picture; the political and social aspects were, in fact, just as relevant. In the appendix on the history of sociography, Zeisel points out that outside Europe several researchers had tried before to employ the methods of participant observation. Yet none of them had raised the question of what social preconditions would have to be met before such an approach could be taken. Of course, researchers wanting to be more than reporters of facts or neutral observers in the community that they study might not always be able to carry out their plan, and obviously, whether or not their plan succeeds depends on more than just their efforts. Resistance to their investigations, misunderstandings, and personal inability of the researcher may contribute to its failure. *Marienthal* does not seem to have encountered any such difficulties. Indeed, one might argue that it was the embeddedness of the researchers into the Social Democratic Labor Movement, as well as the fact that Marienthal was a village whose entire population had become unemployed, that allowed the researchers to succeed in their investigation. Because everyone in the village had become a potential subject, selection of a group interested in the study, or establishing contacts with them, was not

Introduction to the Transaction Edition   *xix*

the problem. The common Social Democratic background shared by the researchers and the majority of their respondents also helped them to overcome potential difficulties. The mutual respect the social scientists and the Social Democrats had for each other encouraged cooperation between the two fields. The research team, for example, discussed their initial plans with Otto Bauer, the leading intellectual of the Social Democratic Party, who persuaded them to abandon a plan to study leisure-time activities of workers in favor of investigating the destructive consequences of being unemployed. Beyond that Bauer called the attention of the young social psychologists to the tiny village of Marienthal as a research site with strategic advantages. On the other hand, an intellectual-turned-politician like Bauer never would have forced the social scientists to withhold or polish results for political reasons. This matching of politics and scholarship has seldom been replicated.

The Socio-Cultural Micro-Environment

As indicated earlier *Marienthal* originally appeared without the names of its authors on the title page. The reason for this was simple. The book was published by the Leipzig-based publishing company Hirzel and appeared in the spring of 1933, just a few weeks after Hitler had seized power in Germany. The publisher asked the authors to omit their names from the title pages to avoid political difficulties because of the Jewish sounding names and the group of authors agreed. Probably they also erased some politically objectionable sentences.[14] The surprising lack of political interpretations in *Marienthal* however could have been the result of the series in which the study appeared: *Psychologische Monographien* was edited by Karl Bühler who advocated strictly academic language, a lesson Lazarsfeld had to learn earlier when his first manuscript submitted to the Bühlers had been turned down because of its political tone.

> [S]he [i.e., Charlotte Bühler] objected strenuously to the tone in which my section on proletarian youth was written. I was, indeed, full of compassion, talking about exploitation by the bourgeois society, and the hortative style of this section was quite different from the rest of the manuscript. I could not deny this fact, and finally rewrote it. None of the argument was omitted, but the whole tone became descriptive and natu-

xx   *Introduction to the Transaction Edition*

ralistic, instead of critical. I have no doubt that this episode affected my subsequent writings and is a contributing factor to the debate on the role of sociology that was later led by C. Wright Mills."[15]

The way Lazarsfeld and his colleagues accommodated themselves to the new political environment was still very different from what others did at this time. Whereas the authors of *Marienthal* abandoned an opportunity to earn a reward, opportunists flattered the Nazis. Even some with family names easily detectable for "Jew-sniffers" tried hard to continue their academic career under the new rulers. For instance Theodor Wiesengrund, who only after his coming to the U.S. became Theodor W. Adorno, even published texts praising Nazi musicians and applied for a membership in Goebbels' newly erected *Reichsschrifttumskammer.*[16]

Although Jahoda, Lazarsfeld, and Zeisel sacrificed in strict professional terms a lot by dissolving their names from their first major publication their renunciation was in accordance with their sociopolitical socialization in Vienna.[17]

All three, and most of their collaborators, came from fairly well-established, Jewish upper middle-class families. They did not deny their Jewishness, but it did not play a major role in their self-awareness before the Holocaust. Their families did not pay attention to Jewish rituals but were assimilated to the Gentile majority. Very different from their contemporaries in Germany these Viennese "non-Jewish Jews"[18] did not encounter a serious religious phase in their early life, as it happened in the cases of Erich Fromm, Walter Benjamin, and others. Vienna's middle-class Jews were predominantly agnostic in religious terms, leaning towards liberalism around the turn of the century and changed their inclination later to the Social Democratic Party. Paul Lazarsfeld was born in 1901, his father Robert was a lawyer and his mother Sophie ran a salon where leading left intellectuals met regularly. One of them became young Paul's mentor and Paul's mother's lover: Friedrich Adler, the son of the founder of the Social Democratic Party in Austria, Victor Adler. Friedrich Adler was a trained physicist who abandoned a job offer at Zurich in favor of Albert Einstein.[19] He became well known during World War I when he assassinated the prime minister of the Hapsburg Empire as a signal for an anti-war upheaval. The court case against Adler and especially his eloquent plea politicized a

Introduction to the Transaction Edition   *xxi*

whole cohort of young people and convinced them to join the labor movement. Paul Lazarsfeld took part in a demonstration in front of the court house and was arrested. After the proclamation of the Republic in 1918 Lazarsfeld not only began studying mathematics, physics, and social sciences, but started a political career too. He published articles in papers of the labor movement, participated in discussion groups, acted in political cabarets, and organized so-called summer colonies where he met Marie Jahoda. They became a couple and married in 1926. The marriage ended in divorce in 1934.

Marie Jahoda was six years younger than Lazarsfeld. Under his influence she began studying psychology at the University of Vienna, where Hans Zeisel, born 1905, attended the Law Faculty to become a lawyer like his father. In addition Zeisel studied economics and volunteered as a sports reporter for the Social Democratic daily *Arbeiter Zeitung*.

Vienna was at this time a seedbed of psychology. Apart from the dominant psychoanalytic school of Sigmund Freud, the rivaling depth psychologist Alfred Adler tried to utilize his competence for social reform, parents education, and educational counseling. Both depth psychology circles did not have a footing in the universities; Freud himself held only an honorary professorship during his lifetime. The university department of psychology, then still part of the philosophy department, was chaired by Karl Bühler who came to Vienna in 1924, accompanied by his wife Charlotte who became the third woman to get a teaching appointment as *Privatdozent* at the University of Vienna. Thanks to the financial support from the municipality of Vienna and due to funds provided by the Rockefeller Foundation, the Bühler couple started a wide-ranging teaching and research program in psychology. Lazarsfeld's mother was a devotee of Alfred Adler, and her son and his friends participated first in Adlerian activities before they entered the Bühlers institute. Lazarsfeld started his career there as the expert for statistics. He never got a regular post in the university but was paid out of the Rockefeller funds.

Besides his doing statistical calculation for everyone at the institute, Lazarsfeld tried to establish a separate division for social psychology. Finally, in 1931, he created with the support of Karl

xxii   *Introduction to the Transaction Edition*

Bühler the Wirtschaftspsychologische Forschungsstelle (Research Branch for Economic Psychology). This small company was modeled after the Viennese Institut für Konjunkturforschung (Institute for Business Cycle Research) which was initially under the co-directorship of Ludwig Mises and Friedrich A. Hayek, and later came under the directorship of Oskar Morgenstern. Both institutes were formally located outside the university and its members had ties to the academic world only as *Privatdozent*. This adjunct position gave its holder the "right to teach" but no regularly paid post in the university. The very German institution of *Privatdozent* functioned as a waiting post for aspirants for a professorship. Someone who wanted to become a professor in Central Europe had to submit a post Ph.D. thesis, pass an examination by a special commission and had to wait afterwards for the next opening of a professorship. Due to the congestions of too many aspirants for too few posts, the waiting period lengthened and only wealthy people could afford it. The Bühlers tried to secure Lazarsfeld such an appointment, but failed due to the increasing anti-Semitic mood in academic circles. As a compensation for this disappointment Lazarsfeld was nominated for a Rockefeller Fellowship for the academic year 1933-34.

In the short time between the creation of the *Forschungsstelle* and the departure of Lazarsfeld to New York the group of still very young social psychologists were tremendously productive in terms of raising contracts, performing small studies, and experimenting methodologically. The *Forschungsstelle* was mainly concerned with what was later called market research. They investigated the habits of consumers of tea, coffee, stockings, shoes, beer, milk, etc., not only in Vienna, but also in Zurich, Berlin, and other places in Central Europe. The surveys were usually conducted by hired *rechercheure*, or data-recall facilitators, at the remuneration of one shilling for every filled-out sheet. After some trial and error, the guidelines for data collection became relatively uniform: Starting with socio-demographic variables, the investigator had to turn to previous and earliest experiences with the product under investigation, followed by a detailed examination of the last purchase, the period of planning the purchase, the genesis of the intention to buy, the time between the forming of the intention and the buying act, and finally expectations with regard to the commodity.

Introduction to the Transaction Edition   *xxiii*

Only few of these investigations were reported in print, most of them were summarized in some pages only for the particular client. After Lazarsfeld's departure, the Forschungsstelle, now under the directorship of Marie Jahoda, was planning to establish a quarterly, called "Sales Barometer," but due to the political circumstances this plan did not work out. From the surviving manuscripts one could learn that the market researchers were still thinking along the lines of Austromarxism, the specificity of Marxism that had omitted the crude dogmatisms of Karl Kautsky and Vladimir Ilyich Ulyanov, a.k.a. Lenin, and implanted into Marxism a sturdy shot of empiricism adopted from Ernst Mach's philosophy of science and his followers in the Vienna Circle of Logical Positivism. Only in such an intellectual environment was it possible to study the selling of soap or the purchase of coffee. The curious researchers gained new social psychological insights and satisfied business clients by the then complete new lesson social class was playing in the interpretation of advertisements and the role it had in the selection of brands.

> Austrian women of the lower classes are extremely antagonistic to any lightening of their household work: they object to centralized cooking in the community houses; they are unwilling to send out their laundry, even though this costs no more than when done at home; they do not care for labor-saving devices – and all because they are afraid that their importance for the husband and family will diminish if they have less to do.[20]

"Proletarian consumers" used cologne only on special occasions whereas the well-to-do used it regularly. Therefore advertisements should address different social strata accordingly.

Much later, Lazarsfeld was criticized for his submissiveness to big business, the market researchers, and advertising industry by the student movement's spokespersons and critical theorists presumptuously rejecting mass culture. Reading the surviving papers from the Forschungsstelle could lead one to a complete different conclusion. The Social Democratic social psychologists detected the integration of working-class people into the market society at a time when their purchasing power was still negligible. To take ordinary people seriously was a core effort by Vienna's Social Democrats, and to stretch this endeavor to ordinary consumers sounds

xxiv   *Introduction to the Transaction Edition*

much more egalitarian than high-brow reasoning about the masses and their vices.[21]

The story of the Forschungsstelle and its market research reveals something different too: the reconcilability of micro and macro approaches in the social sciences. An undogmatic reading of Marxism provided the group around Lazarsfeld with a macro-sociological frame of reference and the purely academic psychology taught by Karl and Charlotte Bühler offered them through their teaching about learning, language, perception, mental development of children, tools for analyzing decision-making processes. Lazarsfeld who loved anecdotes and paradoxical messages once put it this way: his Viennese market research resulted in "the methodological equivalence of socialist voting and the buying of soap."[22] In both cases choices are the core of the action.

Politics destroyed the micro-environment in which those ideas were first formulated and the members of the Forschungsstelle were turned into victims of political repression who narrowly escaped. Lazarsfeld who was urged to return to his Austrian home base after the end of his Rockefeller Fellowship was able to prolong his stay in the U.S. for a second fellowship year. After the final expiration he did not change his place of residence but only his status, "from a distinguished foreigner to an undesirable alien."[23] After some struggle, he got a foothold in the U.S., first as the director of a marginal research project in New Jersey and afterwards as the research director in the then-famous Princeton Radio Research Project, before starting his academic career at Columbia University.[24]

His former wife Marie Jahoda took over the directorship of the Forschungsstelle but shifted again more into politics after the defeat of the labor movement uprising in 1934 and the ban of all Social Democratic organization by the authoritarian regime in Austria. When she used the Forschungsstelle as a cover address for underground activities she was imprisoned, indicted, and finally convicted for illegal political activities. Jahoda spent more than a half year in prison and was released only on condition that she abandon her citizenship and leave Austria. This happened during the summer of 1937. Half a year later, the Nazis took power in Austria and the country became part of the German Reich. If Jahoda would have declined to leave Austria the summer before, the Nazis

Introduction to the Transaction Edition   xxv

would have deported her to a concentration camp which she would not have survived because she was a Jew. Hans Zeisel and others escaped after the *Anschluss* and no member of the Forschungsstelle became a Holocaust victim. Whereas Jahoda stayed in her first country of refuge, England, until the very end of World War II, Zeisel emigrated to the U.S. before the war broke out; initially he worked for market research companies in Manhattan and became a professor of law and sociology at the University of Chicago in 1953. In 1945 Jahoda relocated to New York too and lived there for the next decade, before returning to England.

The Fate of the Book and a Research Program

Surprisingly enough, given the political conditions of the time, *Marienthal* received a warm reception immediately after its appearance. Leading journals reviewed the study of the not very well-known Viennese group. Reviews, written in different languages, appeared in print in journals of more than one scientific discipline. Around a dozen reviews were published in Germany, Austria, Italy, the Netherlands, Belgium, the United Kingdom, and the United States. Even the official German *Reichsarbeitsblatt* published a short and friendly review. The outstanding German sociologist Leopold von Wiese devoted three pages in his *Kölner Vierteljahreshefte für Soziologie* to the study.[25] Nearly half of the reviews accepted the fact that no names of authors appeared on the front page, but the other half searched the book's content to find out the names of its authors. Given the political circumstances of the time *Marienthal* received a fairly warm reception in academic and political circles. However the political conditions in Austria prevented its authors from gaining full advantage of their success and transforming their new reputation into professional promotion.

Only Paul F. Lazarsfeld, whose visible contribution to *Marienthal* was his signing of the introduction, benefited from his work before he left Austria for the U.S. He used several occasions to present the results of the co-operative research whose *spiritus rector* he definitely was.[26] He presented the findings from Marienthal at the International Congress of Psychology in 1932, and he wrote summaries for academic journals.[27] In addition, an American visitor to Vienna published a report about the study in the *Nation* under the

Introduction to the Transaction Edition

telling title "When Men Eat Dogs."[28] Robert S. Lynd, who acted as Lazarsfeld's mentor during his fellowship period in New York, pushed the young Austrian. Lynd's *Middletown in Transition* made extensive use of the findings reported in *Marienthal* and as a consequence Lazarsfeld started not only translating *Marienthal* but wrote his first paper in the U.S. about the methodology used in Marienthal. "Principles of Sociography" never appeared in print because neither truly American journals nor the University in Exile's newly established journal *Social Research* was interested in publishing this article, nor did the translation appear at this time. It was circulated only in a photo-copied version. Nevertheless the methodological reflections must have had some personal value for Lazarsfeld himself because he used this old paper for his "Forward to the American Edition Forty Years Later." (The corresponding quote is on page xiv of this edition.)[29]

Marie Jahoda experienced similar difficulties trading off the recognition earned through *Marienthal* into an occupational reward after her forced departure from Vienna in 1937. Due to the help of British sociologists, especially Alexander Farquharson from the Institute of Sociology in London, she was able to continue her research. She was commissioned to study a self-help project for unemployed miners organized by a group of well-meaning, middle-class Quakers. Jahoda spent some months in Welsh miners' communities and reported her findings in a book-length manuscript which she handed over to the Quaker leader, Jim (later Lord) Forrester. After reading her slightly Marxist interpretation about the difference between real work and surrogate work, according to the view of the miners, Forrester told Jahoda that her interpretation would destroy his lifework. Since Jahoda was deeply indebted to Forrester's help in bringing her family members out of Nazi Vienna, she withdrew the manuscript from publication. It appeared in print only some fifty years later. [30]

In spite of its immediate recognition as a sound and worthwhile study, *Marienthal* disappeared from the scholarly scenery for more than thirty years. Through the 1930s world politics defined other topics as pressing, and in the years after the end of World War II unemployment disappeared from the scene at least for two more decades. No one, neither in Central Europe nor in the U.S. was

Introduction to the Transaction Edition   xxvii

interested in a study that examined the socio-psychological consequences of unemployment. Social problems like this were seen as purely historic subjects.

Marienthal reappeared in 1960 in a series *Klassiker der Umfrageforschung* (Classics in Survey Research), edited by the leading German public opinion pollster Elisabeth Noelle-Neumann. After the publication of the American and English translations in 1971 and 1972, respectively, a reprint of the German 1960 edition in the leading German publishing house Suhrkamp added to the fame of *Marienthal* its wide circulation up to today.[31]

When unemployment recaptured center stage in highly developed countries, social scientists looking for prototypes rediscovered *Marienthal* and the two surviving authors, Jahoda and Zeisel. While Zeisel limited his contributions to some reminiscences about Red Vienna and his socialist convictions[32] Jahoda resumed studying work commitment and unemployment after her retirement as a professor of psychology at the University of Sussex. Over the next thirty years *Marienthal* functioned as a blueprint for successors' studies. Jahoda's contributions about the latent functions of paid work had a lasting effect on students of work and unemployment from different disciplines and a wide range of countries.

Taking *Marienthal* as a case-study in itself one could argue that different factors played a role in its long lasting influence. First, as an empirical research report it attracted attention only when the subject under investigation worried ordinary people and scholars simultaneously, second, as an exemplary text it was attractive for novices and researchers looking for advice, and third, the multifaceted troubled circumstances of *Marienthal's* origin illustrate compellingly that in the social sciences outstanding work can live at the very margins of the scholarly world.

Notes

1. See Anthony Oberschall, *Empirical Social Research in Germany, 1848-1914*, Paris: Mouton 1965.

2. Robert K. Merton, "Socially Expected Durations: A Case Study of Concept Formation in Sociology," in: *Conflict and Consensus: A Festschrift in Honor of Lewis A. Coser*, ed. by Walter W. Powell and Richard Robbins, New York: Free Press 1984, 272.

xxviii Introduction to the Transaction Edition

3. Zwei Jahre später, four-pages long typed fragment in: Paul F. Lazarsfeld Papers, Columbia University's Butler Library Rare Book and Manuscript Division, box 39.

4. Interview with Professor Lotte Schenk-Danzinger by the author, Vienna, June 14, 1988 (transcript in the Archive for the History of Sociology in Austria, AGSÖ, Graz).

5. Paul Lazarsfeld, "An Unemployed Village" in: *Character and Personality* 1. 1932: 148. In an interview conducted shortly before his death Lazarsfeld provided names of collaborators and maintained that the later chancellor of Austria, Bruno Kreisky, was one of his subordinates in Marienthal. Nico Stehr, "A Conversation with Paul F. Lazarsfeld," in: *American Sociologist* 17. 1982 (3): 150-155. There is no independent confirmation for this claim, but one could find other names in the Marienthal files in the Lazarsfeld Papers.

6. Norman K. Denzin, *The Research Act: A Theoretical Introduction to Sociological Methods*, Englewood Cliffs, N.J. : Prentice Hall 3rd ed., 1989, 234ff.

7. Marie Jahoda, "Aus den Anfängen der sozialwissenschaftlichen Forschung in Österreich," in: *Zeitgeschichte* 8. 1981:. 133-141; *British Journal of Social Psychology*.

8. Hans Zeisel, "Zur Soziographie der Arbeitslosigkeit," in: *Archiv für Sozialwissenschaft und Sozialpolitik* 69. 1933 (1): 105. The paragraph from which these quotes are taken seems to have been adjoined after the proof reading, therefore it could be seen as a rejoinder to criticisms by a reviewer or another contemporary commentator (one should bear in mind however that at that time peer review procedures were unknown).

9. Hans Zeisel, "Zur Geschichte der Soziographie," in: *Die Arbeitslosen von Marienthal*, Leipzig: Hirzel 1933, 120.

10. O. A. Oeser, "Methods and Assumptions of Field Work in Social Psychology," in: *British Journal of Psychology* 27. 1938: 352.

11. Marie Jahoda, *Arbeitslose bei der Arbeit. Die Nachfolgestudie zu 'Marienthal' aus dem Jahr 1938*, ed. by Christian Fleck, Frankfurt: Campus 1989, 4.

12. Zeisel, "Zur Geschichte der Soziographie," 1933, 96.

13. Lazarsfeld, "An Unemployed Community," 1932, 147.

14. As a consequence of war related demolitions the publisher's archive did not survive. The story follows therefore from the memories of the authors of *Marienthal*, given at different occasions.

15. Paul F. Lazarsfeld, "An Episode in the History of Social Research: A Memoir [1968]," in: *The Varied Sociology of Paul F. Lazarsfeld*, writings collected and edited by Patricia L. Kendall, New York: Columbia University Press 1982, p. 24.

Introduction to the Transaction Edition xxix

16. Rolf Wiggershaus, *Die Frankfurter Schule: Geschichte, theoretische Entwicklung, politische Bedeutung*, Munich: Hanser, 1986, 180 and 199.

17. It is not without irony to recognize that most of the reviews indicated the names of the two main authors Jahoda and Zeisel and some of the early quotations separated Marie Jahoda-Lazarsfeld from her then husband Paul Lazarsfeld and added his name to make the study a collaborative work of three instead of the two – unmentioned – authors: "Jahoda, Lazarsfeld, and Zeisel 1933". One could find further evidence for the disinterested and "communist" role performance of Lazarsfeld in his practice of publishing articles under the pseudonym Elias Smith because he "considered it more important to publicize the institution than to lengthen my personal list of publications," "Memoir," 45.

18. Isaac Deutscher, *The Non-Jewish Jew and Other Essays,* edited with an introduction by Tamara Deutscher, London: Oxford University Press 1968.

19. Philipp Frank, *Einstein, His Life and Times*, New York: Alfred A. Knopf 1947, 19.

20. Paul F. Lazarsfeld, "Appendix D. Social Prejudice in Buying Habits," undated English written manuscript in Paul F. Lazarsfeld's microfilmed files from his study, reel 1, AGSÖ Graz. Also in Lazarsfeld Papers, Columbia University's Butler Library, box 34, folder 5.

21. Ronald A. Fullerton published two short but insightful articles about Lazarsfeld's Viennese market research activities: "Tea and the Viennese: A Pioneering Episode in the Analysis of Consumer Behavior," in: *Advances in Consumer Research* 21. 1994: 418-21 and "An Historic Analysis of Advertising's Role in Consumer Decision Making: Paul F. Lazarsfeld's European Research," in *Advances in Consumer Research* 26.1999: 498-503.

22. Lazarsfeld, "Memoir," 19. see: Paul F. Lazarsfeld, "Development of a Test for Class-Consciousness," in: *Continuities in the Language of Social Research,* ed. by Paul F. Lazarsfeld, Ann K. Pasanella and Morris Rosenberg, New York: Free Press 1972, 41-3.

23. "Memoir," 39.

24. "History of Communication Research."

25. Reviews appeared in *Arbeit und Wirtschaft* (Austria), *Zeitschrift für Sozialforschung* (Germany), *Kölner Vierteljahreshefte für Soziologie* (Germany), *Archiv für die gesamte Psychologie* (Germany), *Jahrbücher für Nationalökonomie und Statistik* (Germany), *Reichsarbeitsblatt* (Germany), *Mensch en Maatschappij* (Netherlands), *Sociology and Social Research* (USA), *Archivio italiano di psicologia* (Italy), *Revue de l'institut de Sociologie* (France), *Freie Wohlfahrtspflege* (Germany), and *Literarisches Centralblatt für Deutschland* (Germany).

xxx   *Introduction to the Transaction Edition*

26. There is still some quarreling about the true authorship of *Marienthal*. Evidently the book was the result of a collaborative effort even if it is true that Jahoda wrote the main text.

27. Philip Eisenberg and Paul F. Lazarsfeld, "The Psychological Effects of Unemployment," in: *Psychological Bulletin* 35. 1938: 358-390; Boris Zawadski and Paul F. Lazarsfeld, "The Psychological Consequences of Unemployment," in: *Journal of Social Psychology* 6. 1935: 224-251.

28. Robert N. McMurry, "When Men Eat Dogs," in: *Nation* vol. CXXXVI, number 3533, January 4, 1933, 15-18.

29. See for an extensive interpretation: Christian Fleck, "The choice between market research and sociography, or: What happened to Lazarsfeld in the United States?" in: Jacques Lautman & Bernard-Pierre Lécuyer, eds., *Paul Lazarsfeld (1901-1976). La sociologie de Vienne à New York*, Paris: Editions L'Harmattan, 1998, 83 – 119.

30. Marie Jahoda, "Unemployed Men at Work," in: *Unemployed People: Social and Psychological Perspectives*, ed. by David Fryer and Philip Ullah, Milton Keynes: Open University Press 1987, 1-73 and Marie Jahoda, *Arbeitslose bei der Arbeit. Die Nachfolgestudie zu 'Marienthal' aus dem Jahr 1938*, ed. by Christian Fleck, Frankfurt: Campus 1989. See for complementary interpretations of Jahoda's experiences David Fryer, "Monmouthshire and Marienthal: Sociographies of two Unemployed Communities," in: *Unemployed People*, 74-93 and Christian Fleck, "Einleitung," in: Jahoda, *Arbeitslose bei der Arbeit*, vii-lxxii.

31. *Marienthal* became also translated into French, Italian, Spanish, Norwegian, Korean, and Hungarian.

32. Hans Zeisel, "The Austromarxists: Reflections and Recollections," in: *The Austrian Socialist Experiment: Social Democracy and Austromarxism, 1918-1934*, ed. by Anson Rabinbach, Eagle Point: Westview Press 1985; idem, "Zeitzeuge," in: *Vertriebene Vernunft II. Emigration und Exil österreichischer Wissenschaft*, ed. by Friedrich Stadler, Vienna: Jugend & Volk 1988, 328-331, idem, "Die Hälfte des Gespräches, das ich gerne heute mit Paul Lazarsfeld über Sozialismus geführt hätte," in: *Paul F. Lazarsfeld. Die Wiener Tradition der empirischen Sozial- und Kommunikationsforschung*, ed. by Wolfgang R. Langenbucher, Munich: Ölschläger 1990, 31-37.

FOREWORD TO THE AMERICAN EDITION

Forty Years Later

THE STUDY on which this book is based was done in 1930 in Austria, at the time of a depression that was much worse than anything the United States went through. The first thought that may come to mind is that the findings therefore may be out of date and out of place. The substantive problem is still very much with us, of course, although we now talk more generally, about poverty rather than about unemployment specifically. But it could well be that forty years of research have changed our thinking about the effects of unemployment. A brief look at the literature shows that this is not the case.

One of the main theses of the Marienthal study was that prolonged unemployment leads to a state of apathy in which the victims do not utilize any longer even the few opportunities left to them. The vicious cycle between reduced opportunities and reduced level of aspiration has remained the focus of all subsequent discussions. As a matter of fact, this insight was a simultaneous discovery.

When I came to this country in 1933, I began to collect all available publications on unemployment.[1] One Ameri-

---

1. A summary, containing 112 references, was later published with the help of a colleague. Eisenberg, P. and Lazarsfeld, P. F., *The Psychological Effects of Unemployment*. Psychological Bulletin, vol. 35, no. 6, June, 1938.

xxxi

xxxii   *Foreword to the American Edition*

can, E. W. Bakke, went from Yale to England to study "The Unemployed Man," obviously aware that in Europe the phenomenon could be observed more clearly. He too stressed the effects of unemployment on personality:

Loss of feeling of control has important consequences. It causes the worker to feel a minimum of responsibility for his own fate, for responsibility goes with control.[2]

Marie Jahoda reviewed the international literature on children of the unemployed, and together with a Polish colleague I reviewed diaries of unemployed workers that had been collected by the Polish Research Institute in Poznan. The results were all very similar.[3]

With the beginning of recovery, the impetus for such studies waned and World War II practically eliminated them. It was not until the fifties that interest was renewed, and characteristically it came again first from research sites outside the United States. Oscar Lewis described poverty in Mexico and created the term which since remains central—the poverty culture. In the sixties awareness of this notion became widespread due to Michael Harrington's *The Other America*. The following quotation from Harrington's book almost reads like a summary of *Marienthal*, although as far as I can tell no contemporary American writer was aware of our work:

Psychological deprivation is one of the chief components of poverty. . . . And the terrible thing that is happening to these people [the poor] is that they feel themselves to be rejects, outcasts. . . . They tend to be hopeless and passive, yet prone to bursts of violence; they are lonely and isolated, often rigid and

---

2. Bakke, E. W. *The Unemployed Man*. London, 1933, p. 10. The study was part of a program of the Yale Institute of Human Relations. Another part of it was Dollard's *Caste and Class in a Southern Town*.

3. *Children, Young People, and Unemployment*. Geneva: Save the Children International Union, 1933, p. 332; Zawadski, D. and Lazarsfeld, P. F., *The Psychological Consequences of Unemployment*. J. Soc. Psychol. 6, 1935, 224–251.

Forty Years Later   xxxiii

hostile. To be poor is not simply to be deprived of the material things of this world. It is to enter a fatal, futile universe, an America within America with a twisted spirit.[4]

By around 1960, the problem of unemployment and poverty in this country had become closely related to the Negro problem and the search for remedies had become intense. It is not surprising that eventually politics got involved. Herbert Gans has successfully analyzed the turmoil around "Mobilization for Youth." There, basic sociological knowledge was taken seriously. It was not enough to open opportunities for people long deprived; it was imperative to teach them how to utilize their chances. And pursuing a theory of social motivation, the idea emerged that young people should themselves be involved in creating these opportunities.[5]

It is a frequent complaint that social scientists do not replicate their studies to make sure of their findings. Here we are facing a situation where external events inadvertently made for replication. This is one justification for translating our old study. Before expanding on this justification, an interesting blind spot in our monograph should be brought to the attention of the reader. In hindsight it is clear that our findings had important political implications. But they were not brought out in the published text and, if I remember correctly, we were not really aware of them.

In Austria, where this study was done, the institutional response to mass unemployment was the dole. In the United

---

4. Harrington, Michael, *The Other America: Poverty in the United States.* New York, 1963. In a later work William T. Query discussed *Illness vs. Poverty* (San Francisco, 1968):

> When we speak of poverty, we mean something more than material poverty and drain on the economy. The poverty we have in mind is as damaging to civilization as to the economy . . . it is the poverty of self confidence (among the poor) and the image of themselves that slowly results from working below their capacity or not working at all (p. 6).

There is a great neglect of foreign literature by American writers on this topic. Query mentions some Marienthal findings he had learned via the Zawadski paper. From a translation I have gathered that an Italian writer—A. Gatti, "La Disoccupazione come Crisi Psicologia," Arch. ital. di psicol., 15, 1937, 4–28—comes closest to our findings, but we were not aware of each other's works.

Foreword to the American Edition

States it was work relief, the WPA. While the unemployed worker also underwent severe deprivations in this country, he still had some tasks to perform. Under the dole system he is destitute *and* idle. The specific consequences of the idleness component of unemployment are probably the most important aspects of our study and deserve some further comment. On a large scale it is quite probable that part of the success of the early Hitler movement came about because large numbers of unemployed were taken into barracks and kept busy with paramilitary training. This kept the structure of their social personalities intact. Whether this was experienced as personal relief or as national awakening is probably irrelevant. The "boondoggle" of the early 1930s in the United States should get a great memorial celebration one of these days.[6]

The term "breakdown of a social personality structure" is one way to tag the essential finding of *Marienthal.* In the German original, we used occasionally the expression "reduction of the psychological life space." In this country I have suggested "reduction of a man's effective scope."[7] The purpose of a summarizing terminology is to help the reader organize the main details of a study, but sometimes such verbal tags also make one sensitive to new supporting evi-

---

5. Gans, Herbert, "Urban Poverty and Social Planning," in *The Uses of Sociology,* Lazarsfeld, Paul F., et al., eds. New York, 1967. By now the need for a theoretical foundation of all the programs had become evident. The United States Chamber of Commerce appointed a task force on "The Concept of Poverty," which made the following recommendation in its 1965 report:

> Thought should be given to making a comprehensive historical analysis of the theories and concepts of poverty that have been entertained through time. . . . It would provide a philosophical framework within which current ideas could be compared and further evaluated.

6. This is the more important as the 1960's showed a regression in administrative practices. Social assistance programs introduced a great number of practices which were demeaning to the relief population. This is especially well brought out in "Lessons from the War on Poverty," which Robert E. Levine has published with the M.I.T. Press in 1970.

7. Lazarsfeld, P. F. and Thielens, Wagner, Jr., Glencoe, Ill., 1958, p. 262 ff.

Forty Years Later   xxxv

dence. Shortly after I came to this country, I ran into a study by a Newark social agency on the unemployed and illness that reported as follows:

In general the incidence of illness increased with the duration of unemployment. Only with children below the age of six the relation is reversed; their state of health is better in the families of unemployed parents.

This would sound quite paradoxical if it were not paralleled by our own observation that the unemployed men kept almost obsessive order in their own rooms while they neglected their backyard and lost practically all contact with the larger community and its concerns.

For a long time we did not consent to an English translation of our study. Certain aspects of our approach were very naive. We never stated explicitly our sampling procedures and probably never·had very good ones; our typologies were developed intuitively and never checked for their logical consistency. We did not use attitude scales—we hardly knew about them. Many of the standards on which my collaborators and I would later insist in our teaching were neglected. I can excuse all this only by remembering the adventurous pioneering spirit that propelled us; but it made me uncomfortable enough that for a while I refused any offer to publish a translation. And yet we had a very definite methodological program. It is best expressed in two paragraphs the reader will find in this book, but which deserve special emphasis. In the original introduction I expressed dissatisfaction with unemployment statistics, as well as with casual descriptions of the life of the unemployed in newspapers and belles lettres. Then I stated:

Our idea was to find procedures which would combine the use of numerical data with immersion (*sich einleben*) into the situation. To this end it was necessary to gain such close contact with the population of Marienthal that we could learn the smallest details of their daily life. At the same time we had to perceive each day so that it was possible to reconstruct it objectively; finally, a structure had to be developed for the whole that would

xxxvi *Foreword to the American Edition*

allow all the details to be seen as expressions of a minimum number of basic syndromes.

Like all missionaries, we did not feel a need to justify further what the voices ordered us to do. Still the position was pervasive. In his essay on the history of sociography, Hans Zeisel pointed out that the Chicago studies "for some strange reason did not pursue the statistical analysis of their material." From his reading, he could only find a few examples of the quantification of complex patterns. His review ends with a remark that echoes our program:

American sociography has not achieved a synthesis between statistics and a full description of concrete observations. In works of impressive conceptualization—for instance, in *The Polish Peasant*—statistics are completely missing; inversely, the statistical surveys are often of a regrettable routine nature.

The combination of quantification and interpretative analysis of qualitative material is today in the forefront of the research fraternity's interest. It is therefore worthwhile to trace the origin of our position in more detail. The history of our research procedure will help to explicate the characteristics of our specific position. It plays, so to speak, the role of a slow motion movie that shows more clearly how the different parts look, from where they were adapted, and how they fit into new use. After all, it is no coincidence that the original book had a historical appendix. In a way the following remarks can be considered as extending it by treating our own work as an episode in the history of empirical social research.

The best way is to begin with a brief description of the climate in which the plan for the Marienthal study took shape. The Bühlers, in the newly created Psychological Institute at the University of Vienna, had begun to concentrate on the integration of approaches, an effort best exemplified by the important book of Karl Bühler, *Die Krise der Psychologie*. He had become prominent as an introspectionist, and he was also well acquainted with the tradition of

Forty Years Later xxxvii

cultural philosophy, and especially with the thought of Wilhelm Dilthey; in addition, during a trip to the United States, he had come into contact with American behaviorism. His book is an effort to analyze these three sources of psychological knowledge: introspection; interpretation of cultural products such as art, folklore, biographies, and diaries; and the observation of behavior. But the key to Bühler's thought throughout was the need to transcend any one approach or any one immediate body of information, to reach a broad conceptual integration.

It is difficult to say in detail how we were influenced by this ecumenical spirit, but we certainly never missed a chance to show that even "trivial" studies, if properly interpreted and integrated, could lead to important findings, "important" implying a higher level of generalization. Thus, we once summarized a number of our consumer studies by carving out the notion of the proletarian consumer as:

. . . less psychologically mobile, less active, more inhibited in his behavior. The radius of stores he considers for possible purchases is smaller. He buys more often at the same store. His food habits are more rigid and less subject to seasonal variations. As part of this reduction in effective scope the interest in other than the most essential is lost; requirements in regard to quality, appearance, and other features of merchandise are the less specific and frequent the more we deal with consumers from low social strata.

Other studies had significance by the very nature of their topic and the Marienthal study is the most obvious example. Vienna at the time had a very progressive administration under the leadership of the Social Democratic party. The study of working class problems was always in the forefront of our interests. Thus we criticized the then flourishing literature on youth which dealt only with middle class adolescents. We devoted much attention to the problems of working class youth who at that time started work at the age of fourteen. We tried to show that as a result "proletarian youth" was deprived of the energizing experience of middle class *xxxviii*   *Foreword to the American Edition*

adolescence. Consequently, the working class man never fully developed an effective scope and could therefore be kept in an inferior position.[8] The evidence collected to support this point proved good preparation for the Marienthal study.

In all this work certain norms for empirical study were maintained as a matter of course. It would have been unacceptable just to report that x percent of the people did or thought this or that about some topic. The task was to combine diverse findings into a small number of "integrating constructs." At the same time, it was imperative to explicate as clearly as possible the procedure by which such greater depth was achieved. In a paper written in 1933 summarizing the Austrian experience, the following four rules were singled out and amply exemplified:

a. For any phenomenon one should have objective observations as well as introspective reports.
b. Case studies should be properly combined with statistical information.
c. Contemporary information should be supplemented by information on earlier phases of whatever is being studied.
d. "Natural and experimental data" should be combined. By experimental, I meant mainly questionnaires and solicited reports, while by natural I meant what is now called "unobtrusive measures"—data derived from daily life without interference from the investigator.

More description was not enough. In order to get "behind" it, a variety of data had to be collected on any issue under investigation, just as the true position of a distant object can be found only through triangulation, by looking at it from different sides and directions. It is unlikely that I was entirely aware of the rules underlying the Viennese research tradition as it developed. But its structure was close

---

8. For the content of this work see Leopold Rosenmayr, *Geschichte der Jugendforschung in Oesterreich*, Vienna, 1962.

Forty Years Later

xxxix

enough to the surface so that I could articulate it fairly easily when I had leisure here in this country to reflect on our work.

The study was carried out under the auspices of the Austrian *Wirtschaftspsychologische Forschungsstelle,* a name connoting broadly the application of psychology to social and economic problems; the institution was attached to the Institute of Psychology at the University of Vienna.[9] No sociology department existed at the time. Still, the sociological bent of the project is apparent. The introduction tells that we wanted to study "the unemployed community, not the unemployed individual." The main chapter is called "A Weary Community." It seemed to us that the closed rural community has greater resistance against breakdown than the multitude of urban unemployed. I would include here our preference for objective indicators of trends: apple consumption, newspaper circulation, theatrical performances, etc. And we certainly were sensitive to structural effects, although we would refer to Marx and did not even know of Durkheim. I remember the pride I felt when in a parallel study of youth and occupation I could show an inter-city correlation between the occupational structure of a city and the youngsters' occupational plans.

I conclude with a few suggestions for further research. Today, in this country, it is necessary to make finer distinctions: does the vicious cycle between deprivation, squashed hopes, lowered expectation, self-induced further reduction of effective opportunities, apply in the same way to all deprived groups? Individual unemployed men, in a vast, metropolitan area might react differently than the residents of a totally unemployed coal mine area. Recent ethnic immigrants to this country might show a different pattern compared to the native black population. The destructive effect of enforced idleness probably plays a role in other social problems. One of the difficulties, for instance in the reha-

---

9. More on these connections in Zeisel, H., "L'école viennoise des recherches de motivation." Rev. franc. Sociol. IX, 1968, 3–12.

xl   *Foreword to the American Edition*

bilitation centers for drug addicts, is the lack of necessary funds and of administrative machinery to develop a system of work programs.

Today many studies evaluate the effectiveness of the various programs organized through the Office of Economic Opportunities. Evaluation is the better the more provision is made for two elements: careful recording of concrete events as they occur, and anticipatory speculation as to probable effects and barriers. The design of evaluation studies might profit by sharing our experiences with Marienthal.

Finally, I would like to suggest a specific historical inquiry. As far as I know, no one has really studied in detail how the WPA idea developed during the New Deal. Compared with what the rest of the Western world did, it was a spectacular social invention. Did it slowly seep into the relief legislation as the result of a puritan spirit that no one should get anything without work? Was it explicitly formulated as a sociological idea and carried to victory in governmental circles by specific individuals? Why did no major resistance among unions develop, a factor that contributed so disastrously to the maintenance of the dole in central Europe? Much could be learned if a historically trained social scientist would attempt to answer some of these questions.

The substantive part of our study ended with the hope that the tragic chances of our experiment will not reoccur. History has disappointed our optimism. Situations where creative innovations are needed to overcome collective deprivation and its aftermath have multiplied. The more modest hope to express now is for a more effective liaison between social policy and social research.

PAUL F. LAZARSFELD

Columbia University
Spring, 1971

Marienthal

CHAPTER 1

Introduction

How much do we know about the effects of unemployment? There are some statistics available on the extent of unemployment and the amount of relief provided; occasionally these data are given in some detail by age, sex, occupation, and local conditions. There is also a literature on social problems: newspapermen and other writers have most effectively portrayed the life of the unemployed, bringing home their condition through example and description to those as yet unaffected. But there is a gap between the bare figures of official statistics and the literary accounts, open as they invariably are to all kinds of accidental impressions. The purpose of our study of the Austrian village, Marienthal, is to bridge this gap.

Our idea was to find procedures which would combine the use of numerical data with immersion (*sich einleben*) into the situation. To this end it was necessary to gain such close contact with the population of Marienthal that we could learn the smallest details of their daily life. At the same time we had to perceive each day so that it was possible to reconstruct it objectively; finally, a structure had to be developed for the whole that would allow all the details to

1

2   *Marienthal*

be seen as expressions of a minimum number of basic syndromes.

As this report proceeds, it will become clear how we have tried to build up a comprehensive picture of life in Marienthal, while at the same time accommodating complex psychological situations within an objective framework that is supported by relevant statistics. Every path that could bring us closer to our objective was explored. The testimony of the unemployed themselves brought us face to face with the living experience of unemployment: their casual remarks, their detailed response to our questions, the accounts of local officials, the diaries and letters that we came across by chance. We found some of the data already in usable form: the records of the Co-operative Store, of the various clubs, and of City Hall. For the most part, however, we ourselves had to collect the needed data in the form of meal records, time sheets, and observations of many kinds.

In the end, the detailed data were arranged so as to fit the overall impressions we had gained during our stay in Marienthal and our subsequent study of the accumulated data. We tried to reduce the subjective element that is inherent in any description of social phenomena to a minimum by discarding all impressions for which we had no objective support. In this fashion, our basic insights into the effects of unemployment eventually emerged: a diminution of expectation and activity, a disrupted sense of time, and a steady decline into apathy through a variety of stages and attitudes. It is around this thesis that we have grouped both the characteristic main results as well as occasional deviating details.

Our approach was not meant to deal with the problem of unemployment in its entirety. The object of this investigation was the unemployed community, not the unemployed individual. Character traits were given little attention, the whole field of psychopathology was omitted, and only where definite causal links could be traced between past and present did our study touch upon the case history of individuals. Nor will one find broad generalizations. Our

Introduction 3

concern was the unemployed manual laborer in a particular industry, in a particular village, at a particular time of the year. Such an investigation of a particular community has both its advantages and disadvantages.

We want to draw special attention to one limitation of our study because it led to interesting consequences. We were dealing with a community that was totally unemployed. In the absence of comparable studies of partially unemployed communities, it cannot be said with certainty to what extent the unemployed individual in the midst of an otherwise working community—say, in a big town—differs from the unemployed individual who lives in a place where everybody is out of work. However, a careful examination of our data leads to this conclusion: In Marienthal we found no extreme symptoms of mass neurosis, such as have been observed among German vagrants. This might suggest that for various reasons a closed rural community finds it easier to keep functioning over an extended period of time.

On the other hand, the more subtle psychological effects arising from idleness and the hopelessness of the situation were brought home to us, as it were, magnified and in slow motion. This research advantage clearly emerged from interviews and discussions with those concerned with the problem of unemployment, such as social workers, officials, and politicians. A casual observer is apt to see only what is most conspicuous, namely the occasional revolutionary effects of unemployment, or particularly heartrending outbreaks of despair. Our detailed inquiry has led us to see more clearly the paralyzing effects of unemployment, an aspect that might easily elude less systematic observation. Once perceived, however, evidence of these effects found ample support in the experience of the social workers. We repeatedly observed that when we reported our findings, they at first met with a certain degree of hostility but eventually led even the experts to reassess the facts as they had first seen them.

In order to relieve the report itself of its methodological

burden, we now give a résumé of the kind of data eventually at our disposal and the means by which they were obtained:

Family Files: A lengthy record was compiled for each of the 478 families of Marienthal. Each member had a separate file with his personal data, form of unemployment relief, etc. The file also contained all information relating to housing conditions, family life, domestic arrangements, and so forth. In addition, one family diary was kept for us.

Life Histories: We recorded detailed life histories of thirty-two men and thirty women. The importance of these histories lies primarily in their coverage of the individual's entire life. When these people came to speak of the period of unemployment, their narrative was already under way. They found it, therefore, easier to give expression to the experience of being unemployed, since by then they had reported on that part of their life that offered a basis for comparison. Had we inquired directly about their present condition the result would probably have been embarrassed silence or empty phrases.

Time Sheets: Eighty persons filled out a questionnaire outlining the way they spent their time during a given day.

Reports and Complaints: We studied those made over the past few years to the Industrial Commission of the district of Wiener Neustadt, of which Marienthal is a part.

School Essays: Some primary and secondary school children wrote on the subjects: "What I want most of all," "What I want to be," "What I want for Christmas."

A Prize Essay Competition: Some adolescents wrote on the subject: "How I see my future."

Meal Records: Forty families kept records of their meals for one week; records were also kept of the school children's packed lunches on the day before and the day after relief money was paid.

Introduction   5

Miscellaneous Reports: We collected reports on the Christmas presents received by eighty small children; conversation topics and activities in public bars; parents' problems in bringing up their children (from the notes taken in the doctor's consulting room); medical tests; information from teachers on the performance of their pupils; general welfare work undertaken by welfare authorities, the factory, the parish priest, etc; the money spent at the tavern, the barber, the butcher, the horse-meat butcher, the shoemaker, the tailor, the confectioner; and reports from the various political clubs and other organizations.

Statistical Data: These consisted of the account books of the Co-operative Store; loans from the public library; subscriptions to various newspapers; membership figures of clubs; election results; age distribution, births, deaths, marriages, and migration figures.

Housekeeping Statistics: An official from the Chamber of Commerce came to Marienthal for the special purpose of collecting household statistics, but because of technical difficulties he was able to obtain them only for a few families.

To obtain all this data was not enough. If we were to succeed we had to adopt a very special approach: we made it a consistent point of policy that none of our researchers should be in Marienthal as a mere reporter or outside observer. Everyone was to fit naturally into the communal life by participating in some activity generally useful to the community. This proved most difficult in the case of the researcher who actually lived in Marienthal. However, even this problem was solved surprisingly well with the help of all kinds of special projects we launched, such as the following:

Clothing Project: Through private collections in Vienna we managed to procure some two hundred pieces of clothing. After being cleaned and repaired, they were distributed to the population by our research team in co-operation with the official Winter Aid of the Grammat-Neusiedl district. Since children's shoes and warm socks were in particular demand, we supplemented the collection with purchases of some new socks and shoes from our own funds. Previously, one of our researchers had visited one hundred families and asked which pieces of clothing were most urgently needed. These visits gave us unobtrusive access to the home, and enabled us to ascertain the particular needs of the family and discover which member received special attention.

While issuing the clothes we made detailed records of the behavior of the recipients, their reactions to this kind of assistance in particular and to their own predicament in general. Finally, contact with the population was facilitated by Dr. Lotte Danziger's preparatory work in connection with the clothing project; she inspired the confidence to which we owe the copious biographical material the workers confided to us.

Our other projects worked in much the same way. We have listed them below, indicating the information they helped to collect. The members of our research team were active in various functions; their reports appear throughout the study in their original form as they had been received from the inhabitants of Marienthal.

Political Activity: We knew that the active elements of the population were politically organized and, consequently, we sought to establish political contact with them. Since all shades of political opinion were represented in our research team, we were allowed access to practically all organizations. This ubiquity made it possible for us to check the numerous criticisms of local conditions that reached us from different quarters.

Pattern Design Course: Twice a week for two months we gave a course in pattern design. It was open to everyone and in fact some fifty women attended. The significance

Introduction 7

of the course lay in the fact that it satisfied the desire common to all unemployed for some kind of activity, and that during these sessions we learned much about the attitude of the people of Marienthal toward the idleness to which unemployment had condemned them. We obtained the relevant data in the following manner: during the course we told the women we intended to arrange similar courses elsewhere and asked each participant what exactly she had gained from the sessions and what suggestions she had for improving the course, in case it were to be repeated. The course was so popular that eventually it was decided to extend it beyond its original schedule.

Medical Treatment: Each Saturday afternoon two women doctors—one obstetrician and one pediatrician—gave free medical consultation. In urgent cases they also provided free drugs and medicines. Notes were kept of the conversations in the examination room. These medical consultations provided our best opportunity to learn about the medical and economic circumstances of a family, since the very success of the examinations depended on the patient's truthful reporting. Here we also had an opportunity to check on some of the statements made to the welfare worker, which were at times not quite truthful.

Girls Gymnastics Course: In order to establish contact with the young girls, we arranged a gymnastics course. As most of the boys were active in one organization or other, we could gradually reach the majority of the male adolescents through these organizations. The girls had stopped belonging to any organization since unemployment began, and reaching them was more difficult. Eventually, the gymnastics course proved a way of stimulating their interest and bringing them into contact with one of our female researchers.

Parent Guidance: Partly in connection with the medical examinations, partly after lectures, we gave the mothers an opportunity to come to us with the problems they en-

8   *Marienthal*

countered in bringing up their children. Occasionally they took advantage of this opportunity to consult us on other domestic problems as well.

Finally, we reproduce here part of the instructions with which we briefed our research team, to provide them with guide lines for planning their work.

MAIN QUESTIONS OF OUR STUDY

A. *Attitude toward unemployment*

What was the first reaction to unemployment?

What efforts has the man made to find work?

Who has found work outside the district, and by what means?

What work has been substituted for previous employment (e.g., rabbit breeding, farm work, etc.)?

What is the attitude to temporary employment and particularly to the possibility of emigration?

What are the types and phases of attitudes?

What plans do people still have? Are there differences between adults and adolescents?

What are the differences between those at work and those out of work?

What are the attitudes toward the Assistance Board?

What "superfluous" activities are still pursued?

B. *Effects of unemployment*

What are the effects on the physical condition of the population?

What are the effects on the children's performance at school?

What are the effects on criminality?

Are the older or the younger children more affected by their parents' unemployment?

Where work has been resumed, have any difficulties emerged?

Have political differences increased or decreased?

Have attitudes toward religion changed?

Is there a general shift of interests?

Introduction 9

> What changes have appeared in people's sense of
> time?
> Have the relationships of people toward each other
> changed?
> Is there more evidence of competition or of co-opera-
> tion?
> Are there changes within the family?

Preliminary work and discussions began in the autumn of 1931. Dr. Danziger lived in Marienthal from the beginning of December 1931 until the middle of January 1932. Most of the relevant psychological material was collected during that period. Up to the middle of May individual projects were continued, additional observations made, and the statistical material brought together. Only then did we begin the processing of our data, which took us more than six months. During the actual period of research, the team met once or twice a week, mainly to exchange experiences, discuss observations, and make arrangements for the following days. All in all, we spent some 120 working days in Marienthal; the collected material weighed about sixty-six pounds.

Naturally we came no way near to answering all our questions. For example, because of lack of funds, a psychological test of the school children had to be abandoned.[1] On the other hand, certain points emerged during the research work that we had not considered earlier—for instance, the connections between powers of resistance, income, and previous life history. Sometimes a project did not work out the way we had planned. The prize essay competition for the young came to nothing because of lack of re-response, thus bringing out an interesting new feature: the big difference between apprenticed and unemployed adolescents. On the whole our study had its fair share of the

---

Footnotes added by the authors to the present edition are enclosed in brackets to distinguish them from the original notes.

[1. Since then Busemann has tested the influence of unemployment on the performance of school children and reached conclusions that confirm our observations.]

good fortune and bad luck which usually attend such complex field work.

The usefulness of our methods will have to be judged by their results. What place we believe them to have in the development of sociography we have tried to sketch in the afterword to this volume.

CHAPTER 2

The Industrial Village

MARIENTHAL is a small industrial community on the Fischa-Dagnitz river in the Steinfeld district of Austria. A thirty-five minute train ride brings one from Vienna to Grammat-Neusiedel, the nearest railway station; from there it is about a half-hour walk through the very flat countryside. A stranger to the district would scarcely notice the border between Grammat-Neusiedel and Marienthal; the houses disappear and for about three-hundred meters the road is lined on either side with huts. Then we are in Marienthal. The village is as monotonous as the surrounding district. The one-storied houses are long and low, all built on the same pattern. Off the road there are a number of prefabricated huts showing obvious signs of having been erected in a hurry to accommodate the sudden inrush of workers. Only the former manor house, the factory hospital, and the office block have two floors and overlook the other buildings. Behind the houses, along the banks of the Fischa, two big chimneys stand surrounded by long walls, crumbling away in places—the factory.

The Steinfeld soil is not very fertile and the land is difficult to farm. When farmers settled in this vicinity, they did

11

12   *Marienthal*

not have an easy time. To this day they have to struggle hard to eke out a living. Only few can afford to employ temporary labor from Marienthal during the harvest.

Within an hour's walk from Marienthal there are several small villages, similar in history and structure. One is Velm with its knitwear industry, where the girls earn something like thirteen to eighteen Austrian schillings per week.[1] Then there is Goetzendorf with its cotton mill, where production has been severely cut back and where the weekly wages are twenty-eight to thirty-two schillings; Unter- and Oberwaltersdorf with small mills and a similar wage structure; Mannersdorf with its quarry, where the workers take home up to thirty-two schillings per week; and Moosbrunn, where the glass factory has been closed down for some time.

Other communities grew around a market, a church, or a castle; Marienthal grew around a factory. The history of the factory is also the history of the village.

In Marienthal stands a statue with this inscription: "Hermann Todesko, founder of Marienthal." Every schoolboy can tell his story. In 1830 Todesko came to Marienthal looking for a suitable location for a flax mill. The place seemed ideal. The flat land made transport easy, and the small river on which Marienthal was situated—the Fischa-Dagnitz, with its consistently temperate waters that would not freeze over even during a severe winter—could supply power for the factory. The oldest part of the factory arose on its banks, together with a few houses for workers which were quickly occupied by Bohemian, Moravian, and a number of German laborers. Soon Todesko switched to cotton spinning and the factory expanded. New houses had to be built, small shops opened in addition to the factory store, and the village began to grow.

Todesko, master of the village as well as of the factory, felt responsible for its future. His relation to his employees was decidedly patriarchal. True, the wages were low, and

---

[1. One Austrian (1932) schilling (100 groschen) had the purchasing power of approximately forty American (1971) cents.]

The Industrial Village   13

even the children had to work in three shifts of eight hours a day, but in those days nobody was used to anything else. People liked to come to Marienthal; the accommodations were good, and they were sure to make a living for themselves and their children. Dismissals were rare; once settled in Marienthal, the whole family would be employed in the factory. In order to enable the women to go to work, Todesko opened a kindergarten. For the older children he built a school with two hours of formal teaching each day.

During the 1860s he added the looms and the bleaching works. The factory was now a large industrial complex, and thus the patriarchal relationship between the factory-owner and the workers began to disappear. Slowly trade union ideas began to infiltrate Marienthal; it was then that the first workers' organizations were formed. When in 1890 the first strike for higher wages broke out it was quelled by the military. For six weeks the Imperial Dragoons were stationed in Marienthal. When the retreat was sounded, part of the population had already made their peace with them. Some of the soldiers, preferring life in the village to their martial occupation, had married Marienthal girls and become factory workers.

In the 1890s, a new director came to the factory. He ruled Marienthal for several decades, and during his administration the factory made rapid strides. The main products then were blue and pink cotton prints for export to Hungary and the Balkans. In the factory, the patriarchal order was fading out and the workers' organizations grew steadily stronger. By the turn of the century, Marienthal had become a politically active community.

During the First World War production was temporarily diverted to military supplies. After the collapse of the Empire, the factory was completely reorganized. The newly founded workers' council quickly made its influence felt; there were repeated stoppages and bitter industrial disputes. Those were days of turbulent political activity, still talked about in Marienthal. Meanwhile the factory continued to expand. Rayon production was started, and in

14   *Marienthal*

1925 an annex was built to house the new machinery. In the same year, the entire labor force took part in the big strike of the Austrian textile workers. The following year brought the first signs of a serious depression. Between July and December 1926, half the workers were laid off. Nevertheless, 1927, 1928, and the first half of 1929 were not bad years for Marienthal. New machinery was installed and a change to fabrics of greater width was contemplated to maintain production. Employment was at its peak.

This, however, was only a brief period of improvement, a last effort before the final breakdown in the middle of 1929. In July the spinning mills closed, in August the printing works, in September the bleaching plant. In February 1930 the looms were stopped, and then the turbines too came to rest. Only a few days later, amid much excitement on the part of the population, demolition work began.

Only sixty men were kept on to dismantle part of the plant. A member of the workers' council who was assigned to this group voluntarily turned the job down. He did not want to be one of those who were to destroy their old place of work.

Today, only the dye works and the looms are still standing. The bleaching plant and the spinning mills have been pulled down. Even now not all the debris has been cleared away. From their windows at home, the workers look out onto a heap of rubble, dented boilers, old transmission wheels and crumbling walls where once had been their place of work.

Marienthal has a population of 1,486 (712 men and 774 women), of whom 318 are under fourteen years of age.[2] There is nothing unusual about the age structure of Marienthal; it corresponds roughly to that of all Lower Austria, the province in which Marienthal lies. In the following table we show the age groups as a proportion of the total population, compared with the corresponding figures for Lower Austria.

[2. Unless otherwise stated, the date for all statistics is January 1932.]

The Industrial Village 15

		Marienthal per cent	Lower Austria per cent
Pre-school	(0—5)	8	9
School	(6—13)	13	15
Working life	(15—59)	66	65
Retirement	(over 60)	13	11
Total		100	100

The population of Lower Austria is slightly younger than that of Marienthal, which may be explained by the greater number of children in the rural areas. In Marienthal the average number of births between the years 1927 and 1931 was 19.6 per year, the number of deaths in the same period was 12.4 per year. The population, as in the rest of the country, is basically Roman Catholic, though 167 inhabitants—81 men, 54 women, 32 children—belong to no religious denomination.

There are 478 households; the average number of people per home is 3.1. The distribution of households by size is as follows:

	Number of Persons											
	1	2	3	4	5	6	7	8	9	10	11	Total
Number of households	62	121	150	80	41	9	9	4	1	0	1	478
Per cent	13	25	31	17	9	2	2	1	*	*	*	100

The number of households with children under 14 years of age is as follows:

	Number of Children							
	1	2	3	4	5	6	None	Total
Number of households	126	54	20	4	3	1	270	478
Per cent	27	11	4	1	1	*	57	100

All the houses in Marienthal are owned by the Marienthal Trumauer Company. The families have signed a collective lease agreement with the Company. The average home consists of one room and a kitchen, for which the families now pay four schillings per month, when employed formerly, they paid five schillings. For the smaller homes (one room and one anteroom) they pay three schillings per month (formerly four schillings); for the larger ones (one room, kitchen, and one small bedroom) they pay six schillings (formerly seven schillings).

Marienthal has no church of its own; the people go to church in nearby Grammat-Neusiedl. Contacts with the neighboring town are particularly close because many of the tradespeople come from "across the border." In Marienthal itself there are one tavern owned by the factory, one movie house, two horse-meat butchers, one confectioner, one Co-operative Store, one grocer, one barber, and a number of small sundry shops.

A few years ago the members of the Social Democratic Party built a workmen's clubhouse during their spare time. Marienthal has always been politically active; there has long been a great number of organizations and institutions run by the different political parties. On the Social Democratic side are the party organization, a trade union with an affiliated theatre club, the child welfare committee called Children's Friends, the Society of Free Thinkers, The Flame (a cremation society), a cycling club, the Workers' Radio Club, the Workers' Athletic Club, the Wrestling Club, the Young Socialist Workers, the Republican Home Guard, the Workers' Library, the Rabbit Breeders' Association, and the Allotment Owners' Association. On the Christian Socialist side are the party organization, the Christian Women's Association, the Girls' Club, the Boys' Club, and the child welfare committee called Happy Childhood. On the German Nationalist side are the German *Turn Verein* (Athletic Club) and the German *Gesangs Verein* (Glee Club). The last-named societies are gradually being merged with the recently founded local branch of the National Socialist Party.

CHAPTER 3

The Living Standard

THE DAY ON WHICH the fortnightly payments of unemployment relief are made is more important than Sunday. The entire economic life moves in this fortnightly cycle. As far as possible, debts are paid off on that day, and the *Ratenjud,*[1] as the door-to-door salesman from Vienna is called, comes to arrange terms of payment for his goods. Also the main purchases are made for the immediate future, such as flour, potatoes, and lard. On that day the meals are better than usual, and the children look forward to it as if it were a holiday. They feel the cycle poignantly enough in their diet.

The statistics the schoolteacher collected for us give the following picture of the children's packed lunches:

	Day before payment	*Day after payment*
	(number of children)	
Nothing or dry bread	19	2
An adequate packed lunch	19	36
Total	38	38

[1. Literally, the "installment Jew."]

17

18 *Marienthal*

For half the children the packed lunches disappear toward the end of the two-week period, and only on the day after payment do they regain their normal format. It would seem likely that this fluctuation affects also the main meals at home. However, for some families this fortnightly pay day is at times also the date on which unemployment payments are reduced or even stopped altogether, an event, as we shall see, that represents a serious break in the life of the family thus affected.

In Austria payments to the unemployed are regulated by the law of March 1920, and its twenty-eight subsequent amendments. Payments are related to the man's work record, his previous wages, and the size of his family. To be entitled to relief money, evidence must be supplied that the recipient has been employed for a period of at least twenty weeks during the preceding year and that the loss of wages represents a serious threat to subsistence.

The cost of the payments is born jointly by the employer, the employee, and the local labor authority. Payments are made over a period of twenty to thirty weeks. After this, the claim to relief expires; from then on the worker can only draw emergency assistance. The amount of that assistance is at the discretion of the local Industrial Commission, an independent body with official standing. Emergency assistance normally runs to about 80 per cent of regular unemployment relief. It ceases after twenty-two to fifty-two weeks—the precise duration is again determined by the Industrial Commission. From then on, assistance ceases.

There are two rates of regular unemployment relief, the higher for heads of families and unemployed individuals living alone, the lower for unemployed members of families. The higher rate varies between 0.76 and 3.50 schillings per day, the lower rate between 0.72 and 2.30 schillings. The total amount is not allowed to exceed 80 per cent of the last weekly wage.

Claim to relief is forfeited if any work whatsoever is undertaken for pay. Failure to report even casual employ-

The Living Standard 19

ment can result in the Commission taking drastic measures. The following are typical cases in which relief was subsequently withdrawn: a laborer helped to fell trees in return for fire wood; a woman delivered milk and was given some of it for her children; a man made a little money by playing the mouth organ.

The extent to which Marienthal is dependent on relief is shown in the following table:

STATE OF FAMILY INCOME	Number
Unemployed (no member of the family at work)	
at least one member of family drawing unemployment relief or emergency assistance	358
no member of family drawing unemployment relief, either because claims have expired or because ineligible	9
	367
Working (at least one member of the family)	
in Marienthal	22
in Vienna	56
in neighboring villages	15
Total working	93
Drawing other allowances or pensions	18
Total families	478

Three-quarters of the families in Marienthal thus depend on unemployment payments for their livelihood. The majority of the eighteen families living on pensions and allowances are those of retired railroad workers. The twenty-two heads of families who still retain their jobs and make their living in Marienthal itself are the mayor, the parish clerk, three policemen, the tavernkeeper, the midwife, the teacher, the carpenter, the cobbler, two shopkeepers, the butcher, two shop assistants, the postman, and six workers still employed on various maintenance jobs in the factory.

We have already mentioned the wages paid in neighboring factories within reach of Marienthal. They range between thirteen and thirty-two schillings and are at times lower than some of the unemployment relief rates. Because of this low wage scale, the families working in the surrounding area differ little in their standard of living from the unemployed.

The average income of the 358 families receiving unemployment relief is 1.40 schillings per consumer unit per day.[2]

Some families, but especially single persons, are better off. They might have up to 3.38 schillings per unit per day. On the other hand, some families receive no relief money at all; their claims have expired and they are without any job whatever. The lowest relief rate in Marienthal is 0.26 schillings per unit per day.

Henceforth we shall refer to families whose income per unit per day is 0.66 schillings (20 schillings per month) or less as *minimal* families; those with more than 2.00 schillings per unit per day (60 schillings per month) will be referred to as *maximal* families.

Out of the 367 unemployed households, thirty-three (9 per cent) belong to the minimal, and forty-one (11 per cent) to the maximal category. If, however, instead of counting the number of households one counts the more relevant number of individuals in the two groups, their ratio is significantly altered because the minimal households are on the average larger. The income stratification of the unemployed may be shown as follows:

---

2. We define *consumer unit* in the following way: a child below the age of fourteen receives 0.6 units; a youth fourteen to twenty-one years, 0.8 units; an adult woman, 0.8 units; an adult man, 1.0 unit.

In order to give some idea of the purchasing value of the Marienthal incomes, we list here the average prices of some of the more important food stuffs; 1 kg. (slightly more than 2 lb.) flour of inferior quality, 0.65 schillings; 1 kg. of malt coffee, loose (roasted malt, no real coffee), 0.96 schillings; 1 kg. of salt, 0.70 schillings; 1 kg. of dry beans, 0.56 schillings; 1 kg. of horse meat, 1.80 schillings; 1 liter of milk, 0.38 schillings.

The Living Standard

	Households		Individuals	
	Number	*Per Cent*	*Number*	*Per Cent*
Maximal	41	11	59	5
Average	293	80	1024	84
Minimal	33	9	133	11
Total	367	100	1216*	100

*These 1216 individuals in 367 households represent 82 per cent of Marienthal's total population.

This table shows what enables unemployed households to fall into the maximal category. Comparing the number of households with the number of individuals in those households, we see that we are dealing almost exclusively with single persons and a few couples without dependents.

The peculiarities of the households in the minimal category are less clear. First, here are some excerpts from our more detailed records on these minimal families:

Family 001: husband, wife, four children

Because the former employer of the husband failed to make his social security payments, the family lost its claim to relief. In the spring the husband had a temporary job as a slater. Apart from that the family has been living by begging and stealing. The children and the home are totally neglected. The husband drinks; the wife is in prison on a conviction for slander.[3]

Family 273: mother, one child

The mother had become an alien through marriage and thereupon lost her claim to relief. Immediately after the wedding her husband ran away to join the foreign legion. During the summer she does odd jobs and occasionally receives financial support from her parents. The woman leads a lonely life and is very apathetic; she continually quarrels with her relatives.

[3. The Austrian penal code makes slander and even the use of dishonoring curse words a criminal offense.]

22 *Marienthal*

Family 268: husband, wife, three children

The husband is an alien, the wife is working and earns thirteen schillings a week. Occasionally the husband repairs shoes. They own a garden allotment and admit that occasionally they "swipe some coal." The household is tidy but the mood is one of utter despair.

A summary of the thirty-three minimal families shows this picture: twelve are not entitled to relief because they are aliens; nine families, though Austrian nationals, are for other reasons not eligible (formerly self-employed; period of employment less than twenty weeks, etc.); seven families, though receiving relief money, are so large that the amount per member is inadequate; five families sank to the minimal level because the husband ran away and became an alcoholic or a criminal.

Even the officials no longer pretend that it is possible to live on the relief money one may or may not receive. When a cat or dog disappears, the owner no longer bothers to report the loss; he knows that someone must have eaten the animal, and he does not want to find out who. Violations of the fishing laws and even minor thefts of coal from the railway are ignored by the authorities. A woman told us: "I sometimes go to the railway yard to swipe some coal. Once I got caught but they fined me only one schilling. The police are very good about it, and also the people from the railway have come to know me. Everybody knows anyway what poor devils we are; but you have to be careful not to get reported."

When the farmers find that cabbages and potatoes are disappearing from their fields, they hardly ever take action. A young farmer said to us, "What can we do? The poor devils are really desperate."

But not only the minimal families need something to fall back on for their living. The legal opportunities are limited and the yield is small: garden allotments, rabbit breeding, and, as a last resort, people can see the welfare officer and in some cases get permission to take odd jobs for a few

The Living Standard 23

hours. Once in a long while, however, someone in Marienthal turns out to be improbably resourceful. One man, for instance, who knows every plant and animal in the area, who can imitate the call of every bird, established himself—admittedly without a license—as a temporary dealer in "minor livestock." He is an expert in many other things as well, and his help is welcome everywhere. But this type of skill, with an instinct for every possible source of income, is rare. The others have to make do with whatever lies within the law.

There is some common land, owned jointly by the local authorities and the factory, which has been divided up and let for cultivation and rabbit-breeding at a nominal rent of one schilling per year for an area of approximately seventy square yards. This year all the applications for allotments were granted. Now 392 families out of the total of 478 own an allotment, and ninety-four of them own two or more. Although, as will be mentioned later, these allotments are by no means used only for growing produce, the yield of vegetables is considerable: during the summer, fresh vegetables and lettuce; during the winter, onions and garlic and, for a time, even potatoes.

A typical allotment consists of some five patches, about two by six meters each. One patch might be planted with flowers, another with garlic and onions, the third with strawberries, the fourth with cauliflower or turnips, and the fifth with lettuce.

There are in Marienthal thirty rabbit breeders who belong to the Rabbit Breeder Association, and in addition some 150 independent breeders. Depending on the supply of fodder, the number of rabbits (chiefly for home consumption) fluctuates with the seasons. During the winter, when fodder is short, the stock is generally somewhat reduced.

Municipal welfare assistance has almost completely ceased since the village till is as empty as the pockets of its inhabitants. Nevertheless, in 1930 every family received a food parcel for Christmas containing 3 kg. of flour, ½ kg. of margarine, and ½ kg. of sugar. Families of five received

24   Marienthal

two parcels, families of seven got three parcels. The Winter Help campaign alleviated the situation to some extent, and the welfare committees of the various political parties and the child care organizations did the same for their members. Before 1930, the factory issued 50 kg. of free coal to each family at Christmas and distributed small gift parcels. At Easter and Whitsuntide 1931, the local authorities were still able to help out. At Christmas 1931 the factory remitted the rent for December and gave away, according to need, food vouchers for five, ten and twenty schillings. From time to time the factory also issues firewood. The dividend from the Co-operative Society is also due at the end of the year. Consequently, the situation generally eases around Christmas on account of these various small benefits.

The only real remedy, of course, is a return to work. As soon as proper factory work turns up anywhere in the area, it is seized at once. Despite abnormally low wages, the Marienthal laborers often walk for hours to get to work in some factory in the area, and will do any kind of job for the local farmers in exchange for food. It appears that these odd jobs are usually put in the way of those whose claims have expired or who are not entitled to relief—partly out of a sense of fairness, but partly also because earnings that do not exceed the unemployment relief offer little incentive. Naturally, it was difficult to obtain precise answers to questions that concerned the relief payments. One thing, however, is certain; even the most modest opportunity for earning additional income is jumped at by some member of the community.

CHAPTER 4

Menus and Budgets

IN THE PREVIOUS CHAPTER we gave a few figures on the packed lunches of the school children. We now add more data on food and other items in the household budget. They come from three sources—from the forty-one families who kept diet sheets for one week; from interviews during medical consultations, which to some extent provided a check on the diet sheets; and from a number of household accounts kept by some of the families.

If one arranges the 287 (7 × 41) days on the diet sheets according to the number of meals per day, the following distribution is obtained:

Number of Meals per Day	Per Cent of Days
2	2
3	73
4	25
	100
Total days	(287)

The rule then is three meals a day—morning, midday, and evening. Only on two out of every hundred days must two meals suffice; on every fourth day a mid-afternoon "Jause" is added to the three basic meals. Here are the meat days of the forty-one families:

25

Meat Days per Week	Per Cent of Families
0	15
1	54
2	19
3	5
4	7
	100
Total families	(41)

Of the families (54 per cent) who had meat once a week, all had it on Sunday. Those who had meat more than once had it on Sunday and some other days. During the week, fifty-six of the meals eaten by these forty-one families contained meat; thirty-four of the meat dishes consisted of horse meat, eighteen of rabbit stew, two of beef, one of mincemeat, and one of pork. One unemployment man told us that cat meat was also eaten:

"Cats keep disappearing, Only a few days ago Herr H.'s cat disappeared. Cat meat is very good. Dogs are also eaten. But that began already before unemployment. At J. T.'s, for example, they once roasted a dog. A few days ago a man was given a dog by one of the farmers on condition that the animal be killed painlessly. The man went everywhere to find a basin for the blood and finally got one. But he had to promise a piece of the meat in return. The basin belonged to A's family."

The butcher's assistant reported:

"As long as the factory was working, we killed about twelve pigs and some six head of cattle per week. Now we are down to six to eight pigs and one cow. Even these are not bought by people from Marienthal but by those living in the neighborhood who were not our customers in the old days. The people here have changed from beef and pork to horse meat. Previously there was only one horse-meat butcher, but last year another one started up business. Both were doing well at the beginning of unemployment, but after the first few months it turned out that two were too many. The one who had come later survived; the other one had to close down."

Of the evening meals, 85 per cent consisted either of leftovers from lunch or of bread and coffee, drunk regularly at

Menus and Budgets

Type of Evening Meal	Number of Meals	Per Cent
Coffee (mostly black) and bread	132	45
Left-overs from midday	114	40
Freshly made dishes	41	15
		100
Number of meals on time sheets		(7 × 41 = 287)

breakfast.[1] For smaller children milk was added to the coffee, or, alternatively, they were given cocoa made with water. Some families reported that they had not had sugar in the house for two years; to save money they used only saccharine, which, though giving the taste of sugar, has no nutritional value. In some cases, saccharine and sugar were used alternately. It was usually during the second week after relief payments that people turned to saccharine.

Here are the diet sheets of two families. Meals listed are breakfast (B), lunch (L), afternoon "Jause" meal (J), and evening meal (E).

Family 81[2]
Minimal family, 0.57 schillings per unit per day

Family 167
Average family, 0.98 schillings per unit per day

Monday
B: coffee, bread
L: pea soup, *Griesschmarrn*[3]

Monday
B: cocoa, rolls
L: lentils, dumplings

---

1. The Austrian *Wirtschaftspsychologische Forschungsstelle* (see p. xiv above) has just completed a survey on the part played by coffee in the food pattern of the lower income classes. It found that coffee has a dual function. It is considered a food and also a luxury, and for that reason holds a central place in the diet of the poorest classes in particular.

["Coffee" was seldom pure coffee, which, because of high import duties, was quite expensive. Coffee was "stretched" with "fig coffee" (roasted figs), chicory, and, especially for the children, with malt coffee (roasted malt).]

2. When the mother of this family came to the medical consultation with her three children, she told the doctor that the children were not eating properly. She complained that of the little she was able to give them, they usually left a lot untouched. The doctor thought the trouble was connected with the lack of vitamins in their diet.

[3. Cream of wheat with raisins, slightly fried.]

28 Marienthal

J: ———
E: coffee, bread with lard

Tuesday
B: coffee, bread
L: cabbage, potatoes

J: ———
E: cabbage

Wednesday
B: coffee, bread
L: potato soup,
   Krautfleckerln
J: ———
E: coffee, bread

Thursday
B: coffee, bread
L: potato goulash[5]
J: ———
E: potato goulash

Friday
B: coffee, bread
L: soup, potato noodles
J: ———
E: coffee, bread

Saturday
B: coffee, bread
L: potato soup, beans
J: ———
E: coffee, bread

J: coffee, bread with lard
E: lentils, dumplings

Tuesday
B: coffee, bread
L: bouillon cube soup,
   Krautfleckerln[4]
J: ———
E: coffee, *Krautfleckerln*

Wednesday
B: coffee, bread
L: soup, cabbage, potatoes
J: ———
E: coffee, bread

Thursday
B: cocoa, bread
L: soup, cabbage, potatoes
J: bread with lard
E: coffee, bread and butter

Friday
B: coffee, bread
L: soup, *Schinkenfleckerln*[6]
J: ———
E: coffee, bread, horse-meat
   sausage

Saturday
B: cocoa, rolls
L: horse-meat goulash, bread
J: bread with lard
E: horse-meat goulash and
   potatoes

[4. Fried noodles with spiced cabbage.]
[5. Potatoes in paprika sauce.]
[6. Normally, baked noodles with diced ham; here with diced horse meat.]

Menus and Budgets 29

Sunday
B: coffee, white bread
L: soup, sweet noodles

J: ——
E: coffee, white bread

Sunday
B: tea, rolls
E: beef bouillon with liver
    dumplings, meat loaf,
    lettuce
J: tea
E: meat loaf, lettuce, coffee

Although for budgetary reasons it was impossible for us to supervise detailed housekeeping statistics in more than a few families, we present here, to complete the picture, extracts from the housekeeping accounts of an average family over a period of two weeks. At the beginning of this two-week period, immediately before the relief payments, all groceries had in fact been consumed, and at the end of the period the cupboards were again empty except for a little lard, half a pound of salt, and a few pounds of coal. Purchases and consumption during that period were therefore almost identical. Since family budgets at this level of subsistence offer little opportunity for variation, these budget figures, even though they come from only one family and cover only a two-week period, are quite revealing (see page 30).

The figures come from a family of seven (4.8 consumer units: two adults, five children under fourteen). The family received forty-nine schillings relief money for a two-week period, or 0.73 schillings per consumer unit per day (i.e., 0.44 schillings for each child), which is still above the level of minimal families.

Note first that all but six of the forty-nine schillings—that is, 88 per cent of the total budget—went for food. Second, the proportion of carbohydrates is understandably high: 5½ kg. (about 12 lb.) of flour, on top of rice, bread, and rolls. Vegetables, on the other hand, are rare, apparently because of high seasonal prices; the two-week period extended from May 14 to May 27. The small piece of beef with bones was bought for the first Sunday of the period, while the meatless bones were intended for the soup on the second

		Schillings
5½	kg. flour	3.58
1¼	kg. rice	0.80
12	loaves bread	8.00
20	rolls	1.40
28	liters milk	10.64
3	kg. lard	7.20
50	g. oil	0.18
300	g. beef plus some extra bones	0.95
1	beef bone	0.30
1½	kg. granulated sugar	1.78
1	packet saccharine	0.30
6	eggs	0.72
2	kg. vegetables (cabbage, greens, spinach)	1.56
8	kg. potatoes	1.44
2½	kg. beans and lentils	0.74
1	kg. salt	0.07
1	liter vinegar	0.30
	pepper	0.10
½	kg. malt coffee	0.48
¼	kg. fig coffee	0.48
	cocoa	0.20
45	cigarettes	0.45
	lye and soap	1.70
50	kg. coal	4.00
	Total two-week food budget	49.00

Sunday, when obviously there would not be enough money left for meat proper. The regular and relatively expensive consumption of 2 liters of milk per day is also remarkable; it was bought mainly for the children. We noticed time and again, whenever we visited this family, the special concern for the welfare of the children shown by parents who had to forfeit the most elementary amenities of their own.

The following excerpts from the sales records of the Cooperative Store confirm our observations about the changing pattern of consumption. Flour sales rose by 12 per cent between 1928 and 1930; relatively inexpensive, it was used increasingly as a substitute for other foodstuffs. There was also a shift from the more expensive wheat flour to the cheaper rye flour. The sales figures for butter and margarine

Menus and Budgets

show the following development in index form, with the 1928 consumption level equal to 100:

	Butter	Margarine
1928	100	100
1929	69	160
1930	38	192

The counter movement of the consumption index for expensive coffee and for relatively cheaper cocoa was analogous:

	Coffee	Cocoa
1928	100	100
1929	75	118
1930	63	141

Chocolate consumption fell by 57 per cent. The Grammat-Neusiedl confectioner has a similar story to tell: since the beginning of the lay-offs, sales have dropped by 75 per cent. Sunday sales are down from thirty to forty schillings to sixteen to seventeen schillings. In the old days he used to have sixteen or seventeen *torten* for the weekend; now two are enough. The more expensive brands of chocolate are no longer bought at all, only the small ten-groschen[7] bars. While sales of all other kinds of chocolates and sweets have dropped, the consumption of loose chocolate[8] has risen from 5 kg. to 15 kg. a month. Here too, on the day after the relief money is paid out, sales rise steeply. The confectioner thinks that many young men buy chocolate and banana lollipops instead of drink.

To manage an income which averages just one quarter of the normal wages requires careful planning and sophisticated calculation. Some examples may illustrate this.

Frau P. R. has altogether fifty-five schillings relief money per fortnight. Five schillings are put aside for tobacco and occasional meat. Seven-and-one-half schillings go for milk, the rest for other food. Shoes are repaired by her husband. For Christ-

---

[7. One groschen = 1/100 of 1 schilling.]
[8. Broken, unwrapped pieces; cheapest type of chocolate.]

32   *Marienthal*

mas she bought her son a collar for one-and-one-half schillings and spent three schillings on the christmas tree. The grandmother bought stockings and gloves for the children. Her debts at the Co-op came to thirty schillings, but she was able to pay them back out of the year-end dividends.

Frau M. L. always plans her housekeeping very carefully, working it all out with her husband. During the two weeks they spend thirty-five schillings at the Co-op, and that includes coal. She never runs up any debts. When shoe repairs or the like become necessary, the cost is worked out beforehand and the money saved on food. Planning is easier for her because her husband cooperates: "A man is always better at that kind of thing."

Frau N. Z. has three children aged eight, six, and three. The husband worked right up to the time when demolition started; she herself only worked until 1927, which is why her claim to relief has already expired. She finds it hard to manage on twenty-two schillings per week. Milk and bread are paid every two weeks, everything else on the spot. In this way she knows how much there is left to spend. She cannot buy anything on credit because she would not be able to pay it back. What she spends on food comes to twenty-four schillings per fortnight; another six schillings on coal, and six schillings on milk. She bakes her own bread; the few remaining schillings must be kept for shoe repairs.

The ease and accuracy with which the women can account for their money indicates how carefully everything is thought out and how little room there is for emergencies if their families are to survive. It is understandable that under these circumstances the fulfillment of social duties or of the most simple cultural needs is out of the question.

Frau R. told us that thirty-nine schillings relief money is just enough to pay for food and coal. They cannot afford to have their shoes mended and they have had to cancel the newspaper. Now that her brother's relief claim has expired, leaving him without any support, she has to keep him as well, "God knows how." One sister is married and lives in Yugoslavia. Frau R. has written to her for help but so far has not received any money.

Menus and Budgets 33

Frau N. had a similar story to tell. She herself has not been able to go out to work because of her many children. There has been no great change in their income because her husband always earned poor wages. But she has to be much more careful with the money now that the children are bigger. These days it sometimes happens that, just before the relief payment day, the children have to go without food and she has to go and ask her father for some bread.

Difficulties increase as clothes and furniture wear out. One unemployed man reported:

"At first we always thought it would not last that long, and anyway the loss was not so noticeable because we still had things from the old days. But now our clothes are getting threadbare and we cannot afford to buy new ones."

To procure footwear and keep it in good condition is especially difficult:

A mother of three told us how their money was divided up so that everything was paid for immediately, except milk and bread. She spends ten schillings every two weeks on milk and about forty schillings on food and coal. The remaining few schillings go for minor necessities, and there is nothing left for bigger acquisitions. Her seven-year-old boy had to stay away from school for eight days because he had no shoes to wear.

The teacher says, "A twelve-year-old pupil of mine has only one pair of shoes; more exactly, he has a few bits of leather sewn together hanging from his feet. When it rains or snows he cannot leave the house. When he is not at school, his father keeps him home so that he will not damage these miserable remains even more by playing in the street."

The same question turns up in the parents' guidance consultations: How can one stop the boys from playing soccer, so that clothes and shoes will not be ruined beyond repair? The difficulties become almost insurmountable in case of ill health.

34 *Marienthal*

Frau S. tells us that her child is a great worry to her. He is suffering from spine trouble and is obliged to wear a plaster corset. He should be getting extra food, but she just cannot afford it. At first she ran heavily into debt because of the child's ailment. Previously she had to take him to Vienna once a week for treatment and had to borrow the fare that she could not spare from the housekeeping money. For the last two weeks she has been receiving five schillings assistance for the child. Now she has to go to Vienna only once a month, and the fare is being paid by the Assistance Board.

Our medical service, like all our social work, aside from serving its own good purpose is part of our arrangement for collecting needed data. The insights we gained into the health conditions of Marienthal are summarized below.

The state of health of the community, despite its rural environment, has never been particularly good, according to the doctor's reports.

Work in a spinning or weaving mill is not healthy. The dust affects the respiratory tracts and the ear-splitting noise of the machines frays the nerves. People working in such factories are always exposed to the threat of tuberculosis; the doctor stated that in the old days 90 per cent of the Marienthal workers had been potential cases, but the situation had improved, the people had become more healthy. The absence of factory work affecting the lungs and of heavy physical labor, coupled with a greater amount of time spent outdoors, has had a beneficial effect. This was particularly noticeable during the early days of unemployment. To be sure, this applies only to the adults, who had been at work before. That is why children and adolescents show no such off-setting improvement. In addition they, like everyone else, suffer from the aggravating influence of an altered diet and reduced hygienic standards.

In one instance this decline in physical resistance became strikingly apparent, and became the subject of heated discussions. The Marienthal wrestlers, accustomed to winning, were unable to field a complete team at the district championship held in the neighboring village. They no longer

Menus and Budgets 35

had a suitable heavyweight, and even in the middleweight classes showed much poorer general condition than their opponents from other villages.

Our main health data came from two medical examinations of the children. They were conducted partly by our own medical staff during the consulting hours, partly in connection with the relief work undertaken by one of the political parties. The classification of the children's general appearance provides a clue to their state of health. The children under fourteen years of age presented the following picture:

	Per cent
Good	16
Medium	51
Poor	33
Total	100"

The actual conditions in Marienthal are probably worse than these figures indicate, since those who were completely destitute did not bother to come to the examinations.

According to the dentist's examination, only 8 per cent of the children had good teeth, 63 per cent had one to three teeth affected by caries, 29 per cent had more than three teeth affected.[10]

[9. This is one of several tables on which the number of cases was not recorded in the 1932 original.]

10. The relationship between these health findings and the unemployment of the parents is treated in Chapter 9.

CHAPTER 5

A Weary Community

W E HAVE NOW SKETCHED the economic history of Marienthal and its present economic condition. It is time to take a closer look at life in the village. The chief impression is one of blunting monotony. What we were to encounter later in endless variations was already present at the beginning, in a scene both monotonous and still. People are living here who have become accustomed to owning less, doing less, and expecting less than they had considered essential to life in earlier days.

To assess the extent to which Marienthal had been changed by unemployment, we had to learn something about what the atmosphere and life of the community had been like during normal times. People were more than willing to describe Marienthal as it had been when it was still at work.

Frau P.: "Well, it used to be magnificent in Marienthal before, just going to the factory made a change. During the summer we used to go for walks, and all those dances! Now I don't feel like going out anymore."

Frau L.: "I met my husband in Bruck when he was in the army. I went there with our Soccer Club. In those days the whole of Marienthal used to go along when the Club was playing out of town."

Frau S.: "In the old days the children always got lovely things, clothes and toys, everything they wanted. Before Christmas I always went shopping in Vienna."

36

A Weary Community 37

Herr E.: "I often used to go dancing with my wife. There was life in Marienthal then. Now the whole place is dead."

Links with Vienna had been close. Every self-respecting citizen of Marienthal used to go to Vienna with his wife at least once a week, either to the theater or elsewhere. Especially before Christmas, people went to Vienna to do their shopping, and many children were sent to school in the city. Marienthal itself had been teeming with life; the fairs and dances, particularly during the carnival season, soon made a name for the village in the surrounding country as a place where people knew how to live. Marienthal was even the fashion center for the neighboring villages.

The political organizations had been very active. People used to read a lot, entered eagerly into discussions, and enjoyed organizing a variety of events. The focus of this lively community was the factory, which was not simply a place of work. It was the center of social life:

Herr. L.: "When I came back, I did not feel like continuing as a cobbler. I wanted to work in the factory. Life was better there. As a cobbler you sit all day long with the same two or three people; in the factory it's quite different, you have a great many challenges, and when work is over, you're free and can live it up a little."

Frau W.: "Although I had to work harder in the factory, I liked that sort of life. I enjoyed working, and wasn't stuck in one place all the time."

All this has now disappeared. Silence has come to the factory. Somewhere across the empty courtyards one can hear at times the thud of a hammer knocking old bricks out of a wall. That is the last job the factory has to offer.

Opposite the factory lies the large park, which formerly belonged to the manor. The people of Marienthal once were very proud of it. On Sundays they sat on the benches that bordered the drive with its carefully trimmed shrubs, or walked along the well-tended footpath. Now the park is a wilderness; the paths are overgrown with weeds and the

38   *Marienthal*

lawns are ruined. Although almost everyone in Marienthal has enough free time, no one looks after the park.

The Montessori nursery school, which the workers of Marienthal built for their children, had to close down because it could no longer pay the teacher. The toys and games, well wrapped, are stowed in a trunk in the Workers' Club.

At first, the people of Marienthal hoped that all this idleness would simply end before long. Until recently there were repeated rumors of a Czech industrialist who allegedly was interested in restarting the looms. But hardly anyone believes that any longer. Nobody expects a change.

How this general decline affects the various cultural activities of the unemployed is apparent in some of the conversations we had with officers of the cultural institutions of Marienthal. The manager of the Theater Club, for instance, told us:

"The biggest difference between then and now is that the actors no longer have the same kind of enthusiasm. One has to force them to act; because of the misery, their hearts are not in it any longer. Some of the better actors have left altogether. Although they all would have much more time for the theater now, people have lost interest. The Theater Club won't have to shut down, but one has to try much harder to get anything out of the people."

The records of the Marienthal Workers' Library also show a decline in activity. The number of loans dropped from 1929 to 1931 by 49 per cent, although the former borrowing charge has now been abolished. It is primarily the number of readers that has decreased, but even the few who continue to use the library are reading fewer books than before.

Year	Library Volumes per Reader
1929	3.23
1930	2.30
1931	1.60

A Weary Community 39

This decline reflects a falling off of interest and not a lack of books in a library whose potential might soon have been exhausted. Shortly before the factory closed the stock of books had been enlarged by the acquisition of a library from a neighboring village, yet the figures still went down.

It is often assumed that the unemployed do not use their time to further their education, but the problem is not so simple. If one sees in their situation merely an abundance of time and nothing more, then one will probably be surprised by their reduced interest in reading. However, if one views their whole psychological situation and not just one aspect of it, then these figures simply confirm what we know of the basic situation. The people themselves are often aware of this:

Herr S.: "I spend most of my spare time at home. Since I have been out of work I hardly read at all. One doesn't feel like it any more."

Frau S.: "I used to read a lot, I knew most of the books in the library. Now I read less. God knows, we have other problems these days!"

The following pages will show how a number of institutions have been radically changed by the decline of cultural life and how these changes penetrate deeply into the private lives of the unemployed. The area in which this manifests itself most clearly is politics. A leading political functionary of Marienthal reflected the general attitude in these words:

"I used to read the *Arbeiterzeitung*[1] from the first line to the last, now I just flip through it and then throw it away, even though I have more time."

---

1. The central organ of the Austrian Social Democratic Party, whose extensive political section and general intellectual level makes rather high demands on the working-class reader. The Catholic organizations, from whom we could not obtain precise figures because their meetings were always attended by a few people from the rural vicinity as well, showed (according to one official) a similar decline in the number of people who came to meetings from Marienthal.

40 *Marienthal*

The number of subscriptions to the *Arbeiterzeitung* did indeed drop by 60 per cent between 1927 and 1930. This must not, as one might assume, be seen as a simple economy measure, for the *Arbeiterzeitung* had a special subscription rate for the unemployed of only four groschen per copy; it was interest in politics that had declined. The *Kleine Blatt,* of the same political persuasion, but generally geared toward entertainment rather than politics, lost only 27 per cent of its subscribers, and that despite its higher price (ten groschen per copy).

We gained further insight into the specific forms of this decline in interest from the membership figures of certain organizations in Marienthal. Most of these organizations, one must remember, are of a thoroughly political nature and closely affiliated with the respective political parties.

Only the Social Democratic Party possesses an extensive political organization; for the other parties, a focal point is provided by various cultural clubs. For those with a German national bias, for example, it is the German *Turnverein* (athletic club), and, for the older men the German *Gesangsverein* (glee club) that provides this sort of rallying point. They all lost membership between 1927 and 1931: the Social Democratic Party, 33 per cent; the *Turnverein,* 52 per cent; the *Gesangsverein,* 62 per cent.

Since all organizations reduced their membership fees for unemployed members to a nominal level, financial sacrifice cannot have been the decisive factor. This will become even clearer since (as we shall see later) the membership of some organizations actually kept growing. All political organizations suffered heavy losses. Differences in the rate of decline reflect partly the different degrees of party discipline. Discipline was stronger in the Social Democratic Party because of its political tradition, and in the *Turnverein* on account of its semi-military structure. The *Gesangsverein* was the first to suffer, since its members came mainly from the factory's white collar staff, who left Marienthal immediately after the plant closed down.

A Weary Community   41

Particularly when political parties organize charities, people occasionally try to benefit from all sides; a few men had actually become members of both politically opposed organizations. However, contacts within the community were so close that such duplicity was quickly discovered.

It seems that especially among the younger people the few who are still politically active are those who still have work. The local branch of the Young Socialist Workers has thirty-seven members, only seven of whom are unemployed. When one of their officers lost his job, he resigned from his position and decided to give up politics entirely.

The people are very much aware of the decline in political activity. The functionaries of all parties agree that political hostilities among the inhabitants have abated considerably since the period of unemployment began.

This fact, which so curiously contradicts everything that is happening in Germany [in 1932], probably derives from the peculiarly uniform and hence unifying situation in Marienthal. Everyone, whatever his political affiliation, bears the same lot. However, it is also possible that peculiarities in the Austrian national temperament play their part.

In the old days, political fist fights after party meetings were by no means rare. But during the 1932 election campaign for the Provincial Assembly, which throughout the country was conducted with considerable heat, all that happened in Marienthal was the destruction of a few posters. Otherwise the campaign proceded very calmly. It is not possible to foresee whether this tendency toward moderation of the traditional political differences will be upset by new political developments, for instance, by the growth of the recently-founded local branch of the National Socialist Party.

The picture presented by the organizations that have not suffered from the crisis is equally instructive. The socialist *Children's Friends* showed a membership decline of only 25 per cent for the years 1927 to 1931. The membership of

42   *Marienthal*

the *Workers' Cycling Club* remained unchanged, and two organizations even registered considerable growth: the Catholic organization, *Happy Childhood,* and the Social Democratic cremation society, *Die Flamme,* the latter showing an increase of 19 per cent during that period.

It is not difficult to interpret these figures. The last three organizations offer their members more or less direct financial advantages. The cycling club facilitates insurance payments for the bicycles that are being so carefully maintained by their owners;[2] now that no one can afford the railroad any longer, the bicycle remains the last link with the outside world, the only place where one may still find a job. The organization *Happy Childhood* runs a nursery school, and a modest contribution to the cremation society prevents the inevitable disruption of an already restricted budget in the event of death.

The general conclusion is fairly obvious. As privation increases, organization membership becomes less a matter of conviction and more a matter of financial interest. This does not mean that loyalties and convictions have changed, they have merely lost their motivating power in the face of the pressures of the day. It is as if the cultural values invested in the political struggle had been ossified, or given away once again to more primitive forms of conflict.

The election results clearly reveal the political situation:

	*Per cent of population voting**	*Per cent of votes received*		
Elections		*Social Democrats*	*Christian Socialists*	*Communists and others*
1929, Village council	92	80	17	3
1930, National parliament	94	80	17	3
1932, Provincial assembly	92	79	15	6

*In Austria, voting was (and still is) obligatory for those entitled to vote.

---

2. Austrian law requires liability insurance for cyclists as well as motorists.

A Weary Community

The general immobility of the voting structure is remarkable. The few changes are probably less due to ideological shifts than to the emigration of a number of unemployed workers.

The decline from a higher cultural level of political confrontation was accompanied by a rise in more primitive hostilities motivated by personal malice. This shift could be traced with almost documentary precision. We are thinking particularly of the anonymous denunciations of people who had taken on casual work while drawing unemployment relief. The penalty for this offense was often a prolonged cut-off of relief money. Generally, these denunciations were a reaction to a cut in one's own relief money, or an act of personal vengeance. Here is an example of such a denunciation:

Am hereby informing the Industrial Commission that Herr N. N. (exact address) works for a farmer and draws at the same time unemployment relief; he also has chickens and rabbits, and his wife too draws relief money. Others when they are making a little on the side are immediately cut off relief. Those who do not need it, get it; the others can starve.

The number of such denunciations received by the Industrial Commission during the past four years from Marienthal inhabitants is as follows:

	Number of Denunciations	Founded	Unfounded
1928–29	9	6	3
1930–31	28	7	21

The unfounded denunciations have increased in number; the founded ones have hardly changed.

We suspect that social disputes have sunk to a lower level. Whether on the whole the number of hostile acts has increased or decreased is difficult to say since we do not possess any measure of the state of affairs prior to the period of unemployment, quite apart from the difficulties involved in any quantitative statement of this kind.

44 *Marienthal*

However that may be, side by side with these acts of personal malice we found in many critical situations a great solidarity and much willingness to help. A thirty-five year old unemployed man wrote in his diary:

Today the woman next door came over and asked whether she could bring the children a bowl of soup. People are good when times are bad.

In another case, people who themselves had been unemployed for weeks helped the three children of an alcoholic mother keep their heads above water until eventually the National Assistance took care of them.

Various officials who have known Marienthal for a longer period than we believe that the balance of public-spirited and antisocial behavior has on the whole remained unchanged. This fits in with our own general impression. The antisocial impulses that must accompany any existence on the brink of collapse do not come to the surface because of a growing lassitude. As excitement and fatigue cancel each other out, the overall level of solidarity in the community appears unchanged. In Chapter 7 we will observe the changes that have occurred within the family.

In this chapter we have presented the data from which a picture of life in Marienthal can be drawn in rough outline. The following chapters attempt to put into this picture some significant details.

Unemployed men at the corner, Marienthal, Austria, ca. 1931, unknown photographer [possibly Hans Zeisel], Marie Jahoda Papers 41/F-107, AGSÖ Graz

Construction Worker destroying the mill building, Marienthal, Austria, ca. 1931, unknown photographer [possibly Hans Zeisel], Marie Jahoda Papers 41/F-103, AGSÖ Graz

Shop floor, Marienthal, Austria, ca. 1931, unknown photographer [possibly Hans Zeisel], Marie Jahoda Papers 41/F-105, AGSÖ Graz

Mill in Marienthal, Austria, ca. 1931, unknown photographer [possibly Hans Zeisel], Marie Jahoda Papers 41/F-106, AGSÖ Graz

Unemployed men at bridge balustrade Marienthal, Austria, ca. 1931, unknown photographer [possibly Hans Zeisel], published as a front page illustration in Marie Jahoda, Paul F. Lazarsfeld and Hans Zeisel, "Marienthal: The Sociography of an Unemployed Community", Chicago, Aldine, Atherton 1971

Paul F. Lazarsfeld 1929, unknown photographer, Marie Jahoda Papers 41/F-7, AGSÖ Graz

Construction worker destroying the mill building, Marienthal, Austria, ca. 1931, unknown photographer [possibly Hans Zeisel], Marie Jahoda Papers 41/F104, AGSÖ Graz

Marie Jahoda 1929, Jardin de Luxembourg, Paris unknown photographer, published in Marie Jahoda, "Ich habe die Welt nicht verändert": Lebenserinnerungen einer Pionierin der Sozialforschung ed Steffani Engler and Brigitte Hasenjürgen, Frankfurt: Campus 1997

CHAPTER 6

Response to Deprivation

OUR INVESTIGATIONS in Marienthal began with visits to the homes of about one hundred families. The ostensible occasion was to ask them about their particular needs in connection with our proposed distribution of clothing. The observations and interviews recorded during these visits taught us much about the basic posture of the families. Whichever member of the family eventually came to collect the clothes was asked to tell us his life history, which was usually done willingly. These people were then observed in a variety of surroundings: at our courses and at political meetings we talked about them and with them, taking notes of everything as we went along. From these notes and from the special information obtained from meal records, time sheets, etc., detailed descriptions of each family emerged. Here are extracts from our files on two rather typical families.

Family 366: Husband, wife, five children

5.0 consumer units altogether. Husband's unemployment relief: 49 schillings; wife's: 22.40 schillings every two weeks. Hence, total income per unit per day: 1.02 schillings. Have a garden allotment.

The apartment consists of one small room and a big kitchen with livingroom, nicely kept. Despite the lack of

45

46 *Marienthal*

space everything is tidy. The children are clean and well cared for, the mother told us she maintained and mended all their things herself. Nevertheless, the scarcity of clothing has already become acute. With regard to the clothing project, the mother asked whether she could get a coat for her fourteen-year-old son. They sold their radio a few months ago and stopped taking the paper because it was too expensive. The housework took a lot out of her, but sometimes her husband gave her a hand. The children too did their bit.

As to the husband, as long as he was at work he had been all right. He never put up with anything he did not like and always stood up for his rights. However, he had often been forced to change his place of work. He had been in the war, but that was by no means his worst time. In his leisure time he had been the leader of a band, an activity he pursued with all his heart. He still does this at times, but nowadays people just cannot afford to spend money on hearing music. He often used to go to concerts in Vienna. On Saturday evenings he went to the pub. Naturally, all this had now come to an end. He did not believe that things would ever get better in Marienthal. The government was to blame for the misery, therefore it was only fair for the government to support him. On the whole, he did not seem particularly dissatisfied. "One can get along like this as well. Bachelors are better off, they can emigrate. But with a family? . . . I would have liked to give the children an education, but as it is now we are glad we can still give them something to eat." The superintendent at the factory described the man as a particularly able worker.

The husband is a member of the Socialist Party though not much interested in politics. He likes to go for walks and often plays cards at the Workers' Club. His wife attended our pattern drawing course with great enthusiasm and did not miss a single lesson. She even mended her husband's suits. The packed lunch for her children of school age is not different on the day before the relief

Response to Deprivation

payment from the day after (bread and lard). One daughter who had taken various domestic jobs keeps coming back home because she feels happier here. The meal sheet shows that the family has meat (horse-meat goulash) once a week.

These records give some indications of the nature and extent of the reduction of wants: the family has given up their newspaper and radio; the husband does without trips to Vienna and visits to the pub: "One can get along like this as well." They economize above all on food and on the most basic clothing requirements. The higher education of the children, too, has to be sacrificed. At the price of all these restrictions the mother maintains the physical well-being of the children and an efficient level of housekeeping, which, for example, means a good packed lunch for the children every day.

Family 23. Husband, wife, three children

Altogether 3.6 consumer units. Husband's unemployment relief: 47.40 schillings: wife's: 22.40 schillings every two weeks. Hence, income per unit per day: 1.38 schillings. Have a garden allotment.

The accommodations—big room, kitchen, anteroom—are well kept. The children are clean and well dressed. From the clothing project the wife wanted a jacket for her husband. She told us she could not go out to look for part-time work because the children were still too small. Her husband, she complained, does far too little to help her around the house. She does not believe that things will ever be different in Marienthal; she has no plans whatever. But they would get by somehow. Lunch was about to be served; it consisted of beans in gravy.

The husband wanted to become a butcher, but his father forbade it. Whereupon he declared that if he could not become a butcher he would not learn anything at all, and after leaving school went straight to the factory as an unskilled laborer. During the war he had been a prisoner

48   *Marienthal*

in Russia. "I was better off there than anywhere." He could have stayed on "but after all, one belongs in one's own country." Since 1921 he had been living in Marienthal. His idea would have been to go back to Russia, but he was doing nothing about it. "We are still all right for the time being," he said.

As a child at home, the wife had been very unhappy. Her great desire had been to teach needlework, but that was out of the question. At seventeen she had her first child, which soon died. From then on she worked in the factory until it was shut down. She often quarrels with her husband because he does not bother about anything. It was not so bad before the unemployment years but now he was never at home. She so much wanted to go out once in a while. Sometimes she forced him to stay home and went off alone.

The husband spends most of his time at the Worker's Club or reading magazines and novels. He is always in a good mood and therefore very popular with everyone. He is often invited to parties at the pub because he is good fun. At home it is his wife who always has the last word, and she keeps demanding an exact account of how he spends his time. Once she remarked to us: "Somehow we will manage to keep alive; it can't finish us all off." This was very like the husband's statement, "Somehow we we will manage to keep alive," an attitude of resigned composure that foreshadows the possibility of ever greater reductions of all their needs and demands. And as with everyone else in Marienthal, the major reduction cuts into the food budget.

On closer inspection, the various family records suggest a wide range of attitudes. The attitudes represented by the two families described above belong to the middle range, but one soon comes across deviations that call for more subtle differentiation. Let us begin with a divergence toward the positive side:

Response to Deprivation 49

Family 141: Husband, wife, two children

Altogether 3.0 consumer units. Husband's unemployment relief: 42.60 schillings, i.e., 1 schilling per unit per day. Have a garden allotment and keep rabbits.

The accommodations—one room, small bedroom, kitchen—are very well kept. The children are neatly dressed and give the impression of being well cared for. The wife apologized for not having cleaned up yet, although everything looked tidy enough. From the clothing project she wanted something for her nine-year-old boy. For lunch they had rabbit leftovers from Sunday.

Even in his apprentice years the husband had refused to be pushed around by the woman who employed him. During the war he was drafted. When he came up for promotion, he turned it down because he was a convinced pacifist. He had been taken prisoner in Italy and learned the language with great facility. After coming back to Marienthal he married a girl he had known at school. At the factory he soon became the chosen spokesman of his colleagues, and later head of the work council. He always held several different political posts. His idea had been to take a course in tailoring and open his own shop in Vienna. His son, too, is to learn to be a tailor. He is a passionate reader. He would have liked to emigrate to France, but his wife had been against it. Now he was glad that he had not gone, because his colleagues had bad luck there.

He thought the present situation quite bearable. His political job keeps him sufficiently busy because everyone comes asking for his advice, and at any rate they do not expect to starve to death quickly. Colleagues and superiors always held him in high regard. Even today he is still popular everywhere. His attitude is basically optimistic.

The wife brought the children repeatedly to the medical consultations and obeyed strictly all the doctor's orders. She also attended almost all other events in

50   *Marienthal*

Marienthal. There were still a number of good clothes left which the husband himself altered if necessary.

Two things in particular are worth noting about this family record compared with the previous two: the meticulous care given to the household and the atmosphere of contentment that still emanates from the family. This is not a case of muddling through but still a rather purposeful existence. The husband finds the present situation tolerable, is optimistic, and has a number of plans for himself as well as for the education of his son. This family's orientation is toward the future.

The situation is different in the following families whose attitude diverged negatively from the average. This attitude can take two different forms. Family 363 is an example of the first:

Family 363: Husband, wife, four children

Altogether 4.2 consumer units. Wife's unemployment relief has recently been withdrawn, allegedly because the husband should be able to find work on the land. Hence, income at present: nil (according to their statement). They keep rabbits.

The accommodations—a hut with one room, kitchen, and anteroom—are in a terrible state; very dirty and untidy. Children and parents have virtually nothing to wear. Mother and children are dirty; the entire household is slovenly. Unwearable shreds of clothing are littered around. The wife complains that the husband does not help at all and is merely a burden. From the clothing project she just wanted "something warm"—it did not matter for whom.

The wife had a hard adolescence; immediately after leaving school she started work in a factory. She came to Marienthal in 1925. Her marriage used to be better; now she is very unhappy. The husband is not entitled to unemployment relief because he had never worked regularly. Since unemployment began he has not bothered any

Response to Deprivation   51

longer about finding work and leaves everything to the wife. He often goes to the movies and "peddles" all her belongings in various deals, or else he spends his time gossiping and playing cards. The wife even has to chop the firewood herself.

"I couldn't care less now," she told us. "If I could hand the children over to the welfare people I would gladly do so."

The couple is known for its quarrelsomeness. The wife is not too popular. The husband, whom the war left an invalid, is not a bad fellow, just incapable of doing anything. His wife is more intelligent and takes advantage of this.

Here is a type of behavior quite different from that of any family described so far. There is no longer any attempt to weigh different needs against each other and establish a rank order of importance. This family gives the impression of letting itself go completely; there is nothing left to hold on to. The children and the home, usually the last to fall into neglect, are in a bad state.

The next family represents a second type of negative deviation from the average:

Family 467: Husband, wife, two children

Altogether 3.0 consumer units. Husband's unemployment relief: 42 schillings, i.e., 1.0 schilling per unit per day. Have a garden allotment.

The wife was very nervous. When we visited her she immediately started to cry and seemed terribly depressed. The accommodations—one room, small bedroom, kitchen—are very clean and well kept. The clothes of the whole family seemed to be clean and in good condition. From the clothing project the husband wanted clothes for the children. He said: "The most terrible thing is that one can't offer the children anything at all." He was afraid they might become retarded.

52   *Marienthal*

The husband had always been very demanding in life, had wanted to get on and had been full of self-confidence and family pride. He studied and worked and always asserted himself, so much so that when the lay-offs began he was convinced that nothing could happen to him. All during the first months he believed that a man of his ability could not come to grief. During the first year of his unemployment, he wrote 130 applications for jobs, all of which remained unanswered. Now he is at the end of his tether. He told us that he spends half his day in bed now in order to save breakfast and heating. He hardly ever leaves the house. He is in utter despair: "It can't get better, only worse." He hopes everything will collapse. "I could bear everything if only the children could be spared."

There are still some good clothes around from former times, and the wife is very concerned about the children, who are regularly sent to a children's holiday home. The husband sits all day at home and does nothing at all. He has hardly any more contacts with other people.

The behavior of this family is characterized by a high degree of orderliness. Despite their economic decline, a careful attempt is made to run the household as well as possible. But this orderliness is, to an unusual extent, combined with expressions of despair. It is the vestige of an ordered life that distinguishes this family from the previous one; the mood of extreme depression distinguishes it from the main group.

We have presented, so far, four different attitudes. It is not always easy to separate them clearly; in particular, it is not easy to find appropriate names for them. It will be useful therefore, to restate once more the criteria that lead us to place a particular family in one category or another.

The most common basic attitude in Marienthal, the one most visible at first glance, is the one described in the first two family records. It is an attitude of drifting along, indifferently and without expectations, accepting a situation that

Response to Deprivation 53

cannot be changed. With it goes a relatively calm general mood, and even sporadically recurring moments of serenity and joy. But the future, even in the shape of plans, has no longer any place in the thought or even dreams of these families. All this seems to us best characterized by the word *resignation*. Perhaps this does not entirely tally with ordinary usage; normally the word does not convey the transitory picture of contentment which these families sometimes present. However, no other word seems to come so near to describing the reduced demands and the lack of expectations that characterize this attitude to life. In all these cases we found a fairly well-ordered household, and children who were well looked after. If we were to single out from this description the criteria which lead us to categorize a family as *resigned* and summarize them epigrammatically, we would say: no plans, no relation to the future, no hopes, extreme restriction of all needs beyond the bare necessities, yet at the same time maintenance of the household, care of the children, and an overall feeling of relative well-being.

This attitude must be distinguished from that exemplified by family 141: with that type of family one has the impression of greater activity. Their households are as well ordered as those in the *resigned* category, but their needs are less restricted, their horizon wider, their energy greater. Again, it was not easy to find an appropriate expression for this attitude. Eventually, we decided on the word *unbroken* and posited the following criteria for this attitude: maintenance of the household, care of the children, subjective well-being, activity, hopes and plans for the future, sustained vitality, and continued attempts to find employment.

The two remaining attitude groups can both be called *broken*, yet the difference between them is so great that we decided to treat each as a category by itself. The distinction goes to the area in which the state of collapse manifests itself. In family 363 it affected the running of the household, in family 467 it affected the mental outlook.

Let us first look at the latter category, whose outward mode of living is not much different from the resigned but

54   *Marienthal*

unbroken homes. The difference lies in how they subjectively experience this reality. These people are in complete despair, and from this basic outlook the category receives its name. Like the *unbroken* or *resigned* families, they keep their households in order and look after their children. But we must add: despair, depression, hopelessness, a feeling of the futility of all efforts, and therefore no further attempts to find work or to ameliorate the situation; instead, constant comparisons of the present with a better past.

The fourth attitude, finally, differs from the others by the absence of an ordered household. Apathetic and indolent, these families let things take their course without making any attempt to salvage something from the collapse. We call this category *apathetic*. Its main characteristic is complete passivity, the absence of any effort. Home and children are dirty and neglected, the mental outlook is not desperate but simply indifferent. No plans are made, no hopes maintained. The household is in such disarray that it no longer satisfies even the most immediate needs; it becomes completely irrational. In this category we find the alcoholics of Marienthal. Family life begins to disintegrate; quarrels, begging, and stealing are some of the symptoms. Nobody plans for a more distant future, not even for the days and hours immediately ahead. The relief payment is always spent during the very first days without much thought as to what will happen during the rest of the two weeks.

One characteristic of three of the four categories is careful maintenance of the budget. From our conversations with the women, from the way they could remember all the relevant figures, we could tell that they were constantly preoccupied with working out how to spend the little money they had. This is why we were able to give some kind of survey of their budgets in the preceding chapter, although in most cases we could not persuade them to keep household accounts.

But it is equally significant that amid this strict economy we often came across traces of quite irrational spending. Sometimes these "splurges" are probably the first signs of

Response to Deprivation   55

disintegration, but sometimes they simply form the last links with the richer experiences of the past; it is not always possible to decide which. Here are some instances of surprising and seemingly irrational spending.

Flowers are growing on many of the garden allotments, although potatoes and other vegetables are vital; beds that could yield some 160 pounds of potatoes are filled instead with carnations, tulips, roses, bell flowers, pansies, and dahlias. When we asked why this was so, we were told: "One can't just live on food, one needs also something for the soul. It is so nice to have a vase of flowers at home."

A family whose claims to unemployment relief expired a year ago, who for lack of money had to give up, for instance, all sugar and only uses saccharine, whose children are totally neglected, one day bought a cardboard picture of Venice from a peddler, albeit for only 30 groschen.

Another family, living only on emergency assistance, spent good money on mourning clothes after someone in the family died. And a fifty-year-old woman suddenly decided to buy a pair of curling tongs on installments.

Such episodes are frequently bound up with frustrated love for the children. A twelve-year-old boy who, on the day before the biweekly payments appeared at school without even a bite of bread, was given on the following day a salami sandwich, two doughnuts, and a piece of chocolate.

The newspaper vendor who also sells picture books and calendars[1] told us that the sale of picture books had by no means dropped as much as the sale of calendars. He had even gained some new women customers, who on a birthday or other festive occasion and following a sudden impulse, bought a picture book as a present for a child.

Perhaps the first and last examples are to be interpreted as a yearning for some remains of joy; some of the others are possibly symptoms of dissolution. At any rate, these examples should remind us that even the restricted modes of living in Marienthal have not yet reached complete uni-

---

[1. Wall calendars have been traditional in Austria.]

56 *Marienthal*

formity. Nevertheless, the totality of life in Marienthal is correctly described by the patterns that characterize the four basic attitudes. We shall, therefore, now return to them and report on their relative frequency in Marienthal.

Our typology was based on the one hundred families about which we had detailed information from a multitude of sources. We found them distributed as follows among the four types:

Unbroken	16
Resigned	48
In despair	11
Apathetic	25
Total	100

But these families, it must be remembered, are not a cross-section of the community; they were pointed out to us as the ones who needed help most urgently. Later on, when in the course of our inquiry we became acquainted with the entire population, we saw that these hundred families contained all that could be classified as *broken,* but only a fraction of the *resigned* and *unbroken* families. The eleven families *in despair* and the twenty-five *apathetic* families constitute about 2 and 5 per cent of the total population; thus, at the time of our inquiry, roughly 7 per cent had collapsed under the pressure of unemployment. The remaining families divided between *unbroken* and *resigned* in about the same proportion we found among the hundred families.

This impression seems plausible also on other grounds. The range of variation in the mode of living has become very small, and therefore a large number of the hundred needy families were representative of the Marienthal average. If we combine the categories *apathetic* and *in despair* under the heading *broken,* then we may conclude that all the Marienthal families are distributed as follows:

	Per Cent
Unbroken	23
Resigned	70
Broken	7
Total	100

Response to Deprivation

Less than one-quarter of all families are still unbroken. Apart from the pressures of the general situation, there may be another reason why we found so few families in which hope for a way out had been sustained: probably some of the most active and energetic families had already escaped the general fate by emigrating before we came to Marienthal.

The immediate vicinity could hardly be considered as a possible area of emigration; most of those who left permanently went to Czechoslovakia or, if only temporarily, to Rumania. Since 1930, altogether sixty persons have emigrated. Several more foremen can find employment in Rumania, but no one else can make up his mind to go. People have the attitude that it is here they became unemployed, and here they want to wait for better times; who knows how they would fare elsewhere? This attitude is reenforced by the unhappy experiences of some Marienthal families who had gone to France.

On the whole, the younger ones are more likely to leave. Of the sixty people who have left, only thirteen were over forty years old, forty-seven were under forty, twenty-seven under thirty. As one can see, a considerable part of the youth of Marienthal—probably its most energetic and vital part—does not appear in our survey because these young men are no longer there.

If one is guided by the direct impression received from contact with the people, one finds the life of the community even more characterized by an attitude of resignation than the 70 per cent figure would indicate. The *unbroken* and the *broken* elements, each for different reasons, have become less visible, giving rise to the impression of a community completely resigned, which, though maintaining order for the present, has lost all relationship to the future.

Another reason for this overwhelming impression of resignation comes from the degree to which the attitude has affected children and adolescents. Here the resignation is more striking because such an attitude is the last thing one expects to find among youngsters. A few figures will document this situation.

From the children's essays mentioned earlier, on the sub-

58 *Marienthal*

ject of "What I want for Christmas," we calculated the cost of each wished-for present at prevailing prices. Thus we arrived at the following average cost of fulfilling their wishes:

Children from:	*Average Cost of Christmas Wishes* (*in schillings*)
Marienthal	12
Surrounding villages	36

The presents the children of Marienthal wanted cost only about one-third as much as the presents the other children hoped to get. And the children barely dared openly to state even these modest wishes. Almost one-third of the Marienthal essays were written in the subjunctive. They usually started with an introductory sentence like "If my parents weren't out of work . . . " An eleven-year-old schoolboy wrote:

If my parents had any money I would like to have gotten a violin, a suit, poster paints, a paintbrush, a book, a pair of ice skates, and a coat. I did get a winter coat.

A girl of the same age:

I would have asked a lot of things from the *Christkindl*[2] if my parents were not out of work. I did not get anything—only a pair of glasses. I wanted an atlas and a compass.

A nine-year-old elementary schoolboy:

I would have loved to get a picture album. I did not get anything because my parents are ·unemployed.

The children who were not *resigned* before Christmas became so afterwards: for the majority of the Marienthal children, Christmas meant disappointment instead of joy and surprise. The discrepancy between what they wanted and what they actually received was proof of this:

[2. In Austria it is the Christ child who brings Christmas presents, not St. Nicholas.]

Response to Deprivation 59

Compared to the wish, the child received:	Surrounding Villages (per cent)	Marienthal (per cent)
More	18	11
About what was wanted	44	20
Less	38	69
Total	100	100

Many more than half the children from the neighborhood had their wishes at least fulfilled, only a little more than a third received less than they expected. In Marienthal there were sixty-nine out of a hundred children whose wishes had not come true. The discrepancy between wish and fulfillment was greater for the children of Marienthal than for those from neighboring villages, although the level of the Marienthal wishes—whether surpassed, fulfilled, or unfulfilled—was already, as we saw, considerably lower than that of the other children.

The absence of long-term plans is another feature of this basic attitude of resignation. The aimlessness struck us most forcibly when people told us their life history. When recording the life histories of twenty-eight men and twenty-nine women, we also talked to them about their plans for the future. Only fifteen had any plans; most of them think in terms of leaving the place. With one exception, however, they have done nothing to make these plans come true.[3] In reality, even with these few, it is more a matter of wishful thinking than of concrete plans. The adult no longer has any specific designs for the future. To some extent this is also true of the younger generation, as we shall see later.

The almost insuperable difficulties in the way of those who try to improve their situation makes this attitude understandable. And since the influence the people of Marienthal can exert collectively for their improvement is very slight and indirect, the entire community has resigned itself to decline. Again it is the children who provide a partic-

---

3. Remember, however, that sixty people had already emigrated, which means that the people we found in Marienthal were the less energetic ones who stayed.

ularly clear indication of this trend. All grades in the secondary school were given an essay on the subject; "Thoughts about Unemployment." The difference between the children who knew unemployment in their homes and those who came from the neighboring villages was enormous. The latter, too, knew about unemployment. But, whereas the children of Marienthal accepted it with hopeless resignation, the essays of the other children expressed partly their satisfaction at not belonging to the unemployed and outcast group, and partly a fear of one day having to share the same fate.

A twelve-year-old boy from the vicinity of Marienthal whose parents were farmers wrote:

I haven't really thought about poverty and unemployment yet, I am glad that I still get as much to eat as I like.

The child of a worker from the vicinity wrote:

In most countries of Europe there is poverty and unemployment. In many rich families, bread and leftovers are thrown away, and many a family would be grateful if they had their daily bread. And it is the same in every country.

This "would be grateful" phrase was the strongest expression of one's own well-being and of radical dissociation from all those who were less lucky. The children of Marienthal, however, wrote from their experience. A twelve-year-old showed particularly clearly how the knowledge of poverty had already invaded his imagination. He wrote:

I want to be a pilot, a submarine captain, an Indian chief, and a mechanic. But I am afraid it will be very difficult to find a job.

Of course, about one-half of the children could not contribute to the subject more than a few uninvolved, insignificant sentences; but this is a common characteristic of all school essays. Moreover, the frequency of these empty essays was not related to the experience of unemployment. As one can see in the following table, for the Marienthal

Response to Deprivation   61

children it was 47 per cent, for the villages it was 48 per cent. Here is the numerical comparison of how the Marienthal children referred to unemployment in contrast to the children from the surrounding villages:

Reference to Unemployment	Marienthal (per cent)	Surrounding Villages (per cent)
Had not thought about it	16	28
Own experience	37	2
Glad that parents were still working	—	16
Fear unemployment	—	6
Insignificant essay	47	48
	100	100

The older the child, the more unemployment is likely to become a personal problem, even when the child himself is not affected by it. These teenagers are afraid of the future, a sentiment that finds expression in the somewhat naive essay quoted above, with its hedging hopes for a possible career overlaying a real fear of finding any job at all. A thirteen-year-old girl wrote:

I would like to become a dressmaker, but I am afraid I might not find a job and have nothing to eat.

We found this attitude also among the adolescents, except those in apprenticeship.[4] We organized a prize essay competition for the older children on the subject "How I see my future." The poor participation—only fifteen replies came in, although the tempting prize was a pair of new trousers—was in itself indicative of a lack of interest in the question. But the aimlessness was even better documented by those who did participate. Among the fifteen essays, five were written by apprentices. The difference between their replies and the replies of those who did not work was striking. The apprentices developed specific, in-

---

[4. Required schooling on the job, the first stage of an eventually certified, skilled labor or skilled trade.]

62 *Marienthal*

dividual plans for the future in the context of the trade they were learning; the other children expressed only general hopes about a better future, about socialism, where everyone "would have at most 300 schillings per month," about the world revolution that would liberate the oppressed, but nothing about their own particular future.

Here are two examples, representing the two groups side by side. A seventeen-year-old tailor's apprentice writes:

If I am lucky in life I would like to work as a *Geselle*[5] for some years after my apprenticeship, then attend a practical cutting course which should give me a better chance for the future. I then plan to become a cutter in some well-established business. Later I would like to be an independent Schneider-Meister.

A twenty-five year old unemployed young man:

In today's society, this is how I see the future: in today's economic world crisis, where capitalism is creaking at the joints, it won't take very long to shake off the yoke of capitalist reaction. I believe that in the near future capitalism must collapse altogether and give way to socialism, and it would be my greatest joy then to be able to help with the establishment of socialism.

There is no better way of describing the problem of the young generation in Marienthal than by giving an idea of the almost insuperable difficulties met in our attempts to gather information about the adolescent unemployed. The statistics tell us that there are 130 adolescents (aged fourteen to twenty-one in Marienthal, sixty-two boys and sixty-nine girls. Despite numerous attempts we failed to make contact with them except in a few cases. Two small political groups, the Young Socialist Workers and occasionally also a group of young German athletes, were the only ones we could observe, talk to and work with. The great majority of adolescents remained unapproachable. Although we

---

[5. The intermediate stage between apprentice (Lehrling) and master (Meister).]

Response to Deprivation 63

brought in a sports doctor for the boys and organized a gym course for the girls, they just would not come. They disappeared and just "hung around." The leaders of the two youth groups confirmed that their problem, too, was getting hold of the young people.

Among both children and adolescents an attitude equivalent to resignation is very apparent. It is because this attitude is in such marked contrast to what we normally expect from childhood and adolescence that resignation, in the sense we have described it, seems to the outsider so much the basic attitude of Marienthal.

But there is also a second reason. Both a desire and an ability to forget become very apparent, especially whenever a large number of Marienthal people gather together. We do not suggest that getting together in adverse circumstances must necessarily strengthen optimism and cheerful sentiments. But wherever we had a chance to observe such gatherings in Marienthal, this was undoubtedly the case. We have, for instance, notes taken by one of the unemployed on our instructions in the Workmen's Club. Here is his report for December 15:

Toward 6:00 P.M. most of those present—there were eighty-six—left the Club and went home for supper. After 6:00 P.M. the first ones came back and sat around the stove to warm themselves. A little later some more of the younger people and some older men arrived. Today nobody seemed in the mood for more card playing. One of the older men started talking about the good old days when there was still enough to eat and drink. Then he continued: when he was still a young man he used to go poaching with his colleague practially every night. Often they did not even need a shotgun, for the hares just ran between their feet, and all they had to do was to close their legs and the hare was caught. There was much hilarity when he told them how he had once seen a ghost: he tried to throw himself on the apparition but it slipped through his hands; from that day on he stopped poaching. Everyone started to laugh and a young man asked why he hadn't told the story right after it had happened. If he had, Marienthal would now be a place of pilgrim-

64   *Marienthal*

age. When they asked why such things did not happen anymore, the old man said that today's youngsters are no good and do not believe in anything, but he could swear that what he told them was the plain truth.

Then a second man began talking. Yes, in the old days everything was possible. One night he too had been out with his friend, catching bustards. There too, one had to be very careful. He and his colleague each had a big sack, a mirror, and a lantern, for the whole thing had to be done at midnight. They set up the mirrors, let the light of the lantern fall on them and then began to make noises. The bustards aroused by the noise ran to the mirrors and were caught in the sacks. Then they took their catch home. At home he made various attempts at crossbreeding; today, he said, he still had a beautiful cross between a bustard and a goat; the guinea fowl that he had running about at home were the result of it.

When people started to laugh incredulously, a younger man immediately began to tell his adventures: he had been on an expedition with a naturalist in the jungle, and there he had to brave many a terrible danger and adventure. One day, it was already rather dark in the forest and they were just about to put up their tent for the night when out of nowhere a huge tiger appeared. Both men stood there trembling all over, when suddenly, without even thinking about it, he rolled up his sleeve and thrust his arm right down into the tiger's throat, who happened at that moment to open his jaws. Turning the tiger inside out and outside in, he then he picked up by its head a snake that was lying around and started to beat the tiger with it so hard that he got up on his hind legs, begging with his front paws for the beating to stop and promising never to molest them in the jungle again.

Suddenly someone shouted, "Let's go home now, otherwise we will be black with lies before it's even midnight." At 11:00 P.M. the Club closed down.

The notes covered a period of five hours. Reminiscing about better days gone by did not embitter people or make them angry about today. They enjoyed, at least in their thoughts, being far removed from their cares and miseries. The descriptions of the "good old days" were enriched by

Response to Deprivation

fantasies; above all they wanted to laugh and enjoy themselves.

Other notes from the Workmen's Club give similar pictures. Again and again one is struck by the external equanimity and the way time, which has lost its value, is spent. The next chapter will deal more specifically with the curious role of time in the unemployed community.

CHAPTER 7

The Meaning of Time

ANYONE WHO KNOWS how tenaciously the working class has fought for more leisure ever since it began to fight for its rights might think that even amid the misery of unemployment, men would still benefit from having unlimited free time. On examination this leisure proves to be a tragic gift. Cut off from their work and deprived of contact with the outside world, the workers of Marienthal have lost the material and moral incentives to make use of their time. Now that they are no longer under any pressure, they undertake nothing new and drift gradually out of an ordered existence into one that is undisciplined and empty. Looking back over any period of this free time, they are unable to recall anything worth mentioning.

For hours on end, the men stand around in the street, alone or in small groups, leaning against the wall of a house or the parapet of the bridge. When a vehicle drives through the village they turn their heads slightly; several of them smoke pipes. They carry on leisurely conversations for which they have unlimited time. Nothing is urgent anymore; they have forgotten how to hurry.

Toward noon, when the traffic in Marienthal reaches its modest peak, the movements of the people in the roughly three-hundred meters stretch of the village's main street presented the following picture, when we counted for (for

66

The Meaning of Time 67

one hundred of them) the number of times they stopped on their way:

Stops on Main Street	Men	Women	Total
3 or more	39	3	42
2	7	2	9
1	16	15	31
0	6	12	18
Total	68	32	100

Almost two-thirds of the men interrupted their walk at least twice; only one out of every ten walked to his destination without stopping. The women presented a strikingly different picture: only about one-sixth of them stopped on two or more occasions. As we shall see later, they have considerably less time on their hands.

From our concealed position at a window we also attempted, watch in hand, to gauge the speed of movement on this leisurely village street. Here are the walking speeds of the fifty people who were observed while covering a reasonable distance without stopping:

Speed of Walking miles per hour	Men	Women	Total
3	7	10	17
2½	8	3	11
2	18	4	22
Total	33	17	50

Since for every 100 persons walking in the street there were always about thirty simply standing around, the average speed of movement was extremely low. Once someone trotted past; it turned out to be the village idiot.

Time in Marienthal has a dual nature: it is different for men and women. For the men, the division of the days into hours has long since lost all meaning. Of one hundred men, eighty-eight were not wearing a watch and only thirty-one of these had a watch at home. Getting up, the midday meal, going to bed, are the only remaining points of reference. In between, time elapses without anyone really knowing what

68   *Marienthal*

has taken place. The time sheets reveal this in a most graphic manner. A thirty-three year old unemployed man provided the following time sheet for a single day:

A.M.

6–7	Getting up.
7–8	Wake the boys because they have to go to school.
8–9	When they have gone, I go down to the shed to get wood and water.
9–10	When I get back up to the house my wife always asks me what she ought to cook; to avoid the question I go off into the field.
10–11	In the meantime midday comes around.
11–12	Empty.

P.M.

12–1	We eat at one o'clock; the children don't come home from school until then.
1–2	After the meal I take a look at the newspaper.
2–3	Go out.
3–4	Go to Treer's (the shopkeeper's).
4–5	Watch trees being cut down in the park; a pity about the park.
5–6	Go home.
6–7	Then it's time for the evening meal—noodles and semolina pudding.
7–8	Go to bed.

Compare this with the time sheet drawn up by a Viennese metalworker, still employed:

A.M.

6–7	Get up, wash, have breakfast.
7–8	Take the streetcar to the factory, read the newspaper on the way. Start work at 7:30.
8–12	Factory.

The Meaning of Time

69

P.M.

12–1	Half an hour's lunch break. Stay at work and eat a packed lunch.
1–4	Factory.
4–5	Take the streetcar home, finish reading the paper, have a wash, then tea.
5–6	Lie on the sofa and talk to my wife about various things.
6–7	Fetch the children from the playground.
7–8	Evening meal.
8–9	Political party meeting.
9–10	Empty.
10–11	Go home, go to bed.

For an unemployed man the day lasts 13½ hours, for a worker, 17 hours. The few leisure hours the employed worker enjoys after his eight-hour shift are carefully disposed of and incomparably richer and more active than the many hours forced upon the man out of work. Waking the children certainly does not take up a whole hour. Treer's shop (where he spends 3:00–4:00 P.M.) is only three minutes from where this man lives, and the distance from the park to his home which he covers in the hour between 5:00–6:00 P.M. is about 300 yards. What happens in the intervals? Every time sheet tells the same story. A thirty-one year old former unskilled laborer gives us the following data:

A.M.

6–7	Slept.
7–8	Took the boy to school.
8–9	Walked to the railway.
9–10	At home.
10–11	Stood on the corner outside the house.
11–12	Ate.

P.M.

12–1	Slept.

70 *Marienthal*

P.M.

1–3	Went for a walk to the Fischa [the river that flows through the village].
3–4	At Treer's.
4–5	Went to fetch the milk.
5–6	Played with the boy.
6–7	Had evening meal.
7–8	Went to bed.

It is always the same: when he fills out his time sheet, the unemployed worker can recall only a few "events." Between the three reference points of getting up, eating, and going to bed lie intervals of inactivity hard to describe for an observer and apparently also difficult to describe for the man himself. He merely knows that "in the meantime midday comes round." And it is when he attempts to describe this "in the meantime" that the curious entries on the time sheet occur; activities that cannot take more than five minutes are supposed to fill an entire hour. This manner of filling up the time sheet does not stem from a low level of intelligence among these workers; the much more difficult task of keeping household accounts was competently handled. An unemployed man is simply no longer capable of giving an account of everything he has done in the course of the day. Apart from the already mentioned main reference points, the only other activities that can be named and listed are the few that still retain some significance: washing the boys, feeding the rabbits.

Nothing else that happens bears any meaningful relation to existence. In between the few genuine activities, in those intervals characterized by the entry "in the meantime midday comes round," there is mere inactivity, a complete lack of any sensible employment of time. Everything that occurs happens as if it were unintentional. Some insignificant trifle or other determines how the next half hour will be spent. It is, in fact, so trivial that the man is scarcely conscious of it; if he has to give a report of it later, he finds that it has long since slipped his mind. He hears some slight noise outside

The Meaning of Time

71

in the street and goes out; a moment later the noise is forgotten. Nevertheless he remains standing outside until some other trivial impression prompts a further move.

The account of how thirty-one-year-old Franz P. spent one morning provides a characteristic example of this aimless drifting around:

8–9   I got up at eight o'clock, washed, had breakfast and went out in front of the house.

9–10   A former shopmate of mine came past and I talked to him.

11–12   Went for a walk, came across one of my friends' children, and chatted about school and the Montessori (nursery) school.

11–12   Came home and read the paper.

The following remarks, added to this questionnaire, show that the workers are conscious of the futility of spending their time in this way: "What should you do with your time when you're out of work?" Or a reference to the past: "I used to have less time to myself but do more for myself." Or, "Now that we are unemployed, we no longer have any chance of keeping busy."

The significance of the remark: "I used to do more for myself" becomes particularly clear when one recalls the way in which the Viennese metal worker spent his free time. The realization that free time is limited urges a man to make considered use of it. If he feels that he has unlimited time at hand, any effort to use it sensibly appears superfluous. What he might do before lunch can be done equally well after lunch or in the evening, and suddenly the day has passed without it being done at all.

It was not easy to gain an overall picture from all the time-sheets submitted. Because these sheets were filled out in the way we have already described, it was impossible to make use of the hourly divisions as we had intended. Where an hour was no longer experienced as such, there could be no point in summarizing the sheets on an hourly basis. We finally decided to treat each half of the day as a unit and to

72   *Marienthal*

characterize it according to the principal way in which the man spent his time.

The men, for the most part, passed their time in idleness. The chart quoted earlier is typical. We distinguish between this sort of inactivity and the half-days spent in the Workmen's Club, although nothing very different takes place there. It is simply a different setting. The distinction, nevertheless, seems important. The very fact that a man resolves to go to the club and actually goes there indicates a certain goal directedness, a determination to do something that is completely lacking in the first group. Finally, there are still occasional half-days when something is being done simply because the needs of the household require it; wood has to be chopped and water fetched, shopping has to be done and things have to be repaired. A man of forty writes:

P.M.

2–3	Lay on the couch and glanced through the newspaper.
3–4	Chatted with the neighbors.
4–5	Looked at the rabbits at 4:40 and brought some water into the kitchen.
5–6	Waited for supper with the children.
6–7	Had supper, and the children went to bed.
7–8	Talked to my wife.
8–9	By 8:30 we were in bed.

Where helping in the house as a response to the demands of the moment was of short duration, the half-day was categorized as "inactivity and minor household work." Where the half-day was distinguished by a fair amount of household activity, it was labeled "major household work," as for the thirty-five-year-old man who wrote:

A.M.

7–8	Got up at seven o'clock, had a wash and then took the children to school.
8–9	Fed the rabbits and cleaned out their hutch.

The Meaning of Time

9–10	Went to the store.
10–11	Peeled the potatoes and helped my wife.
11–12	Went to fetch the children from school.
P.M.	
12–1	Had lunch.

We have allowed a separate rubic for looking after the children, although it is doubtful that this activity made such exclusive claims on the fathers' time as the sheets would indicate. Nevertheless there were several sheets where a whole half-day was summed up by the remark "went for a walk with the children," or "as my wife was out doing the washing, I kept an eye on our five-month-old baby."

Finally, there are some men who filled their day with various activities that are of no direct relevance to the household. It is mainly the political functionaries and the relatively small number of handymen who belong in this category. The following table gives an overview of the way in which one hundred men spent their time in the morning and afternoon:

	Morning	Afternoon
Idleness		
Sitting at home, going for a walk, standing around on the street, etc.	35	41
Workmen's Club		
In winter playing cards or chess, in fine weather sitting around and chatting	14	16
Inactivity and minor household work		
Fetching water, going shopping, etc.	31	21
Major household work		
Collecting and chopping wood, keeping an eye on the children, working in the vegetable field allotments, mending shoes, etc.	12	15
Looking after the children	6	5
Minor activities		
Radio, handiwork, etc.	2	2
	100	100

Idleness rules the day. The considerable extent to which youth shares the general inactivity is indicated by the records of how those present at the Workmen's Club over a period of six days passed their time principally by playing cards and chess.

Men	*Average Daily Attendance at Workmen's Club*
Up to 21	17
22 to 35	53
35 and up	10
Total	80

If we compare these figures with the age structure of Marienthal as a whole, the high proportion of youngsters and young men in the Workmen's Club stands out. This may be because the younger men help less around the house than the older ones, and the communal life in the club has more to offer them.

The only fairly regular activities of the men of Marienthal are collecting fire-wood, looking after their little field allotments for raising vegetables, and, in many cases, looking after their rabbits. This partial return to an agricultural existence, which the Marienthal industrial worker was able to make, distinguishes him from the urban unemployed and alleviates his position to some extent.

It is difficult to ascertain the length of an unemployed worker's day in Marienthal, since direct observation is impossible and information not readily supplied. Spending a long time in bed—only too easy to understand in winter when fuel is scarce—is apparently felt to be in some way shameful. From the imprecise personal statements we were able to obtain, we arrived at an average waking day of 13 hours for men and 14½ hours for women.

The term "unemployed" applies in the strict sense only to the men, for the women are merely unpaid, not really unemployed. They have the household to run, which fully occupies their day. Their work has a definite purpose, with numerous fixed tasks, functions, and duties that make for regularity. The following tabulation of the principal activities of one hundred women shows how very differently

The Meaning of Time   75

their mornings and afternoons pass compared with those of the men.

	Morning	Afternoon
Housework	75	42
Washing	10	8
Attending the children	6	12
Minor household activities (sewing, etc.) and idleness	9	38
	100	100

Here is a typical account of a woman's day:

A.M.

6–7	Get dressed, light the fire, prepare breakfast.
7–8	Wash and get ready, dress the children and take them to school.
8–9	Wash up, go shopping.
9–10	Tidy the rooms.
10–11	Start preparing the meal.
11–12	Finish cooking the meal and have lunch.

P.M.

12–1	Do the washing-up and clear up the kitchen.
1–2	Take the children to the kindergarten.
2–5	Sewing and darning.
5–6	Fetch the children.
6–7	Have supper.
7–8	Undress the children, wash and put them to bed.
8–10	Sewing.
10–11	Go to bed.

So for the women the day is filled with work. They cook and scrub, stitch, take care of the children, fret over the accounts, and are allowed little leisure by the housework that becomes, if anything, more difficult at a time when resources shrink. The different significance of time for the unemployed man and his wife is brought home by occasional minor domestic conflicts. One woman writes:

Although I now have much less to do than before, I am actually busy the whole day, and have no time to relax. Before, we could

76   *Marienthal*

buy clothes for the children. Now I have to spend the whole day patching and darning to keep them looking decent. My husband tells me off because I'm never finished; he says he sees other women out chatting on the street while I'm at it all day long without ever getting through. He simply doesn't understand what it means to be always mending clothes for the children so that they don't have to be ashamed of themselves.

Another woman:

Nowadays we are always having rows at lunchtime because my husband can never be in on time, although he was as regular as clockwork before.

Thus the men do not even manage to keep to the few fixed times that remain, for punctuality loses meaning when there is nothing in the world that definitely has to be done.

Watching the women at their work, it is hard to believe that they used to do all this on top of an eight-hour day in the factory. Although housekeeping has become more difficult and time consuming for them, the purely physical effort involved before was nevertheless much greater. The women know this and remark on it. Nearly all the accounts of their lives mention the fact that their housework used to keep them up late into the night after a day at the factory. But nearly all of these accounts also contain a sentence such as this: "If only we could get back to work." This wish would be understandable enough on purely financial grounds, but it is repeatedly qualified by the disclaimer that it is not merely because of the money:

If I could get back to the factory it would be the happiest day of my life. It's not only for the money; stuck here alone between one's own four walls, one isn't really alive (Frau A., age twenty-nine).

The work is easier now than it was in the factory days. I used to be up half the night doing the housework, but I still preferred it (Frau R., age twenty-eight).

It used to be lovely in Marienthal before, just going to the factory made a change (Frau M., age thirty-two).

Since the factory closed down, life is much harder. You have to rack your brains to think what to cook. The money doesn't go

The Meaning of Time 77

far enough. You are shut up inside all day long and never go out anywhere (Frau S., age thirty-seven).

I would go straight back to weaving at once if I could; I really miss the work (Frau P., age seventy-eight).

So the women want to return to work despite the greater work load, and not simply for financial reasons. The factory widened their sphere of existence and provided them with social contacts they now miss. But there is no evidence that the women's sense of time has been disrupted in the way it happened with the men.

Finally, once again looking at the village as a whole, we noticed a change in the general rhythm of time. Sundays and holidays have lost much of their significance. The librarian, for instance, reports that although book borrowing used to be particularly heavy on Sundays and holidays in Marienthal as everywhere else, this periodic increase is now scarcely perceptible. The biweekly payments of unemployment relief dictate the rhythm of the community; they have taken over the role of Sunday and the end of the month. Only the children still show considerable adherence to the weekly cycle, and this is partially communicated to the rest of the family.

The seasons of the year, on the other hand, make themselves felt more strongly. The end of the need for lighting and heating, the relief afforded by the produce of the garden allotment, and the possibility of occasional work on the land have attained a significance that they did not normally have in the household of an industrial worker.

So both the general pattern of life and that of the individual show that the people of Marienthal have gone back to a more primitive, less differentiated experience of time. The new circumstances do not fit any longer an established time schedule. A life that is poorer in demands and activities has gradually begun to develop on a timetable that is correspondingly poor.

CHAPTER 8

Fading Resilience

W_{E HAVE DESCRIBED} the state of affairs in Marienthal at the time we were there. But even if the people with their altered sense of time scarcely notice its progress any longer, the months go by and the foundations on which their life still rests are crumbling gradually and irresistibly away. The question is, how long can this life continue?

Since we have seen only the present, one brief moment of history as it were, we have no direct answer. Yet it is this long-term development that poses the real question that constantly forced itself upon us in Marienthal. We are, of course, unable to foretell the future itself, but we did perceive some dynamic symptoms already present in the cross-sectional view of the community that was open to us.

First, however, we shall take another brief look at the past. It appears that the closing of the factory in 1929 produced a definite shock effect. All at once life was completely altered. At the beginning, the women were reduced to panic. How were they to manage the housekeeping money? Who can keep house with an income suddenly reduced to one-quarter of its former size? Many a woman who today has learned how to manage her relief money, had, at the beginning of unemployment, run up debt after debt.

Fading Resilience

79

"From our very last pay envelope I bought my husband three expensive pocket handkerchiefs!" one woman told us. Now she laughs about it; it was such an unnecessary purchase. And none of these women would at first understand that they were all in the same predicament together. "When it began, I thought my husband was the only one who couldn't find work, and I kept sending him off to look for some."

At first, the men thought it would be intolerable to sit around at home merely looking on. We remember the man who sent off 130 applications for jobs in the early months of unemployment. This year he has not written a single one; now he is more worried about the amount of money spent on postage. By now conditions have become much worse; supplies are exhausted, clothes are worn out, the relief payments have been further reduced, and for many people all assistance has expired. Nevertheless, everyone's first reactions were more desperate and irrational.

The president of the Theater Club told us:

In 1929 we only put on four productions. In those days people were in a state of alarm; they all suddenly thought they were going to starve to death. Now everybody has got used to it. In 1930 we put on as many as ten productions.

In those early months, a feeling of irrevocability and hopelessness had a much more paralyzing effect than economic deprivation itself. The Wrestling Club disbanded, but reconstituted itself the following year. The same thing happened to the Workers' Soccer Club—closed down one year, reopened the next.

As time went by, the shock effect began to ebb. Life, as we saw earlier, has reached stability on a somewhat higher level than the first weeks of unemployment allowed people to expect. But the crucial question is: will it *remain* stable?

Let us see which of our data can contribute to an answer. To begin with, economic conditions are constantly changing, and changing for the worse. This is a direct consequence of the unemployment relief laws. After a certain time, unemployment payments are superseded by emergency relief, which in turn is gradually reduced, and can eventually be stopped altogether. But reduced relief payments are only one cause of the deteriorating economic situation. The process is significantly accelerated by the wear and tear on all personal belongings. There is no allowance for their replacement or even for their repair in the carefully balanced budget of a Marienthal household. The moment will come when shoes and clothes, repeatedly mended, finally reach the stage where they can no longer be repaired. Crockery breaks and cannot be replaced. A case of illness will plunge a whole family into debt.

That wear and tear did not raise greater havoc earlier is due to the fact that people had unusually large stocks of materials, especially textiles, which they used to get from the factory for next to nothing. Even now, many families still have some odd pieces of material from which something can be sewn when the need arises. The children's clothes suffered most, of course, and where no more material was available, the parents would take some of their own clothing that was still wearable and decent and have it cut down into coats and other clothing for the youngsters. The lack of underwear, as revealed by the clothing inventory we took of three typical families, is severe. Towels and bed linen suffer less from wear; there are still pillows with lace trimmings, wedding presents that have seen little use. But today most of the women are already busy converting their bed linen into things for the children.

In all three families for which we have detailed data, the children were better provided with clothes than the adults. The women have a ready explanation: it is the children who first benefit from any charity action (public or private). Furthermore, adult clothes can be converted into children's, but not the other way around; and finally it is the children who are cared for most. As a result, the state of children's clothing is relatively good, while the adults often lack the most minimal necessities. Following are some of the details from one of the three inventories.

Fading Resilience

81

Family No. 363: husband, wife, and five children

Clothes: eleven boy's shirts (six of them made by the mother from the father's old shirts); eight pairs of boy's underpants; six pairs of knitted underpants; four knitted undershirts; eighteen small children's shirts and combinations; six handkerchiefs; one man's rowing vest; twelve soft collars;[1] two white petticoats with lace trimmings (one of which was already being refashioned); one woman's blouse; one pair of woman's knitted underpants.

In the kitchen we found only three forks and one lone knife. Since the family had not eaten meat for weeks, this shortage was not too bothersome. The same family's earthenware stock-pot had recently been broken, so they were using a saucepan. However, this saucepan had already been in service for eighteen years and had been soldered on countless occasions. It now leaked and it was doubtful whether it could be soldered again.

As economic conditions deteriorate, how will the attitude of the people of Marienthal change? It will be useful to refer back here to the four categories into which we divided the population according to their basic attitude. Following is the average income per consumer unit in each of these four attitude categories:

		Schillings per Month
Unbroken		34
Resigned		30
In despair	Broken	25
Apathetic		19

This table is not only significant for the connection it establishes between a family's attitudes and its economic situation; it also allows us to foresee at approximately what point the deterioration of income will push a family into the next lower category. In Chapter 4, we summarized the basic differences between these four attitude groups, and we know already that this difference of approximately five

---

[1. To be buttoned to a collarless shirt.]

82   *Marienthal*

schillings a month[2] means the difference between being still able to use sugar or having to cook with saccharine, between having the children's shoes repaired or keeping the children at home, between occasionally having a cigarette or having to pick up butts on the street. But this difference means also the difference between being unbroken, resigned, in despair, or apathetic.

These figures may have no validity beyond Marienthal. In places where not all people are pushed out of work at the same time, neglect and despair may set in at an earlier stage, when the level of income is still higher. Comparison with the surrounding world seems to play its part in matters of mood and attitude.

Thus economic deterioration carries with it an almost calculable change in the prevailing mood. This fact is intensified by the concomitant decline in health. There seems to be a close relationship between income and health, as became clear when the medical examination records of the school children were related to the economic condition of their families. In the following table, the health of the children is rated from good to poor:

Children's Health Rating	Per Cent of Fathers Still Working
Good	38
Average	9
Poor	0

Of the fathers of the children still in good health, 38 per cent were still at work; of the fathers of the children with a "poor" rating, all had lost their jobs. This is an instance of how unemployment undermines the powers of physical resistance.

People gradually lose contact with their tradition of vocation and work; in their place they have acquired a new vocation—being unemployed. Again, it is neither the young people, for the apprenticeship they had just finished was still fresh in their minds, nor the old people, with their deeply

---

[2. Five schillings, it will be remembered, were the equivalent in purchasing power of about two (1971) dollars.]

Fading Resilience

ingrained vocational tradition, who are the first to be disaffected. The danger of losing their work tradition, their working mentality, is greatest for that middle-aged group of men who were already once before torn from their jobs by the first World War.

We were given evidence of this change quite incidentally. At the head of the time sheets we had distributed in Marienthal, the men were asked to state their age, sex, and occupation. To this last item the response was as follows:

	Per Cent
Stated their occupation	25
Stated their occupation with the comment "now employed"	23
Wrote "unemployed"	52
Total	100

Half of those who stated their occupation without further comment had recently finished their apprenticeship, while most of the remainder in that group were over fifty; only about one-tenth were between twenty-one and fifty. It is the intermediate age group that stops identifying with its former occupation as time goes by. Gradually, these men become a class apart from all others—the unemployed. This is a social psychological development the full significance and complexity of which will probably become clear only in more settled times.

One of the questions of major import for the future of the unemployed individual is how unemployment affects his personal relationships. We have already seen how political passions subsided and how personal animosity increased, and we have seen also evidence of touching helpfulness, especially toward children.

Our knowledge about the effect of unemployment on relationships within the family came primarily from our conversations with the women. We are aware that this source by itself does not give the whole picture, since their remarks are often engendered by isolated incidents in the family. The evidence would have been better if we ourselves had

84 *Marienthal*

observed family life over a long period of time; this, however, was not possible. Nevertheless, there is merit to those isolated reports, precisely because they select the incidents that stick in the women's minds as worth reporting. We shall draw no conclusions but simply point to possibilities.

In some cases, unemployment improved the relationship between husband and wife; for example, in one family mentioned earlier, the new situation forced the husband to give up drink. Often, too, where the wife used to feel neglected by her husband, his presence at home is now a source of satisfaction. One woman wrote:

By and large I get on better with my husband now he is out of work, because he helps more around the house and keeps an eye on the children. He was not so good with the first children we had as he is with the younger ones.

One has the impression that a tendency to improve the relationship already existed on the woman's side, and their common predicament strengthened a latent inclination by removing obstacles on the man's side.

On the other hand, in some marriages that had developed quite normally before, the new pressures created nervous tension and occasional quarrels. The best example of this was found in the diary that one unemployed worker kept conscientiously from the beginning of his unemployment. It showed how new and unfamiliar tensions and minor conflicts darkened the relationship between the man and his wife without, however, ever really destroying their basic understanding. Both spoke of one another with the greatest respect and affection when talking to a third party. Here is an entry made not many weeks after the onset of unemployment:

Going into the forest with Martha [his wife] to collect some wood. The best, the only real friend one has in life is a good wife.

A few days later:

Fading Resilience

85

Martha, that most faithful life companion, has just accomplished a feat worth recommending to all for imitation; she has managed to prepare an evening meal for three adults and four children for only sixty-five groschen.

A few weeks later:

I am condemned to silence but Martha is beginning to waver. Today was pay day; after settling our debts at the shop we simply did not have a penny left. Icy silence at home, petty things disrupt the harmony. She did not say good night.

A few days later:

What strangers we are to each other; we are getting visibly harder. Is it my fault that times are bad, do I have to take all the blame in silence???

Family 178 provides an example of the same development. The wife wrote:

We sometimes have quarrels at home these days, but only minor ones, mainly when the boys go on wild hikes and ruin their shoes.

Finally there are cases where family relationships are seriously impaired as a result of unemployment. Yet a closer examination might reveal that these marriages were not exactly happy to begin with. A tense situation might have decisively deteriorated under the pressure of privation. One woman said:

He had always been fairly quarrelsome, even during the old days at the factory, but his colleagues liked him and simply looked the other way when they saw him fly into a temper. Now things are worse, of course, because he takes it all out on the family.

Another woman:

I often quarrel with my husband because he does not care about a thing any longer and is never at home. Before unemployment it was not so bad because the factory provided a distraction.

86   *Marienthal*

A third woman related how her husband used to drink and get on badly with her, adding:

Hardship has made our rows more frequent because our nerves are on edge and we have so little patience left.

On the whole, it seems, improvements in the relationship between husband and wife as a result of unemployment are definitely exceptional. Generally, in happy marriages minor quarrels appear to occur more frequently than before. In marriages that were already unsettled, difficulties have become more acute. Tendencies already latent in a marriage are thus intensified by external circumstances.

Relationships between parents and children were illuminated during consultation hours of the Parents' Guidance Service that we incorporated into the medical consultations. We did not get the impression that Marienthal had more problem children than other communities, and this was confirmed by the school teachers. The typical complaints were more about the children ruining their shoes by playing soccer, and the like. Both from our consulting hours and our direct observations we had the impression that parental authority has not suffered in any way. The family continues to perform its educational function as well or as poorly as it did before unemployment began. Thus personal relations proved to be more resilient than relationships toward work or social institutions.

We are approaching the end of our report. We were able to survey quite precisely the material resources available to the people of Marienthal and the manner in which they disposed of them. We saw how economic pressures have slowly but relentlessly increased. We have traced their effects and the ways in which the unemployed confronted them. Their demands on life are continually declining; the circle of events and institutions in which they still participate keeps contracting. Whatever energy is left is concentrated on preserving this narrowing sphere of existence.

Fading Resilience

87

We found a characteristic indication of this process of contraction in the way people's sense of time became disrupted, losing its value as an ordering influence on the passing of the day. Only personal relationships seemed to remain essentially intact. We have distinguished four basic attitudes: the predominant one is *resignation;* a more active one we named *unbroken;* and two deteriorated forms we called *in despair* and *apathetic.* As we look back at these two forms, it now appears that they are probably but two different stages of a process of psychological deterioration that runs parallel to the narrowing of economic resources and the wear and tear on personal belongings. At the end of this process lies ruin and despair.

In the following passage we describe our impressions from a visit to a family typical of the last stage before catastrophe, which was as far as our investigation of Marienthal took us:

We arrived on a Sunday to find the family in no way prepared for our visit. On entering, the following scene presented itself. The father was sitting on a low stool with a pile of worn-out children's shoes in front of him that he was trying to mend with roofing felt. The children were sitting together motionless on a box, in stockinged feet, waiting for their shoes to be finished. The father explained with embarrassment, "You see, this is my Sunday job. On Sundays I have to patch the shoes up a bit so that the children can go off to school again on Monday." He held up the completely dilapidated shoes of the eldest boy. "I just don't know what I can do with these. On holidays he can't go out of the house any more."

We took stock of the household. It was extremely clean and seemed well cared for: the mother's and children's clothes were spotless. The father, it is true, was wearing a completely worn out shirt and a heavily patched pair of trousers. In drawing up the family's inventory we found that this was all he possessed. His jackets and other trousers and his overcoat had long since been converted into coats and trousers for the children. He said, "I don't have to go out, but the children must go to school." The remainder of this reduced set of possessions was found to be in excellent order. The children's shirts were held together

88   *Marienthal*

with tape, and their summer dresses were wrapped up in an old table cloth and well preserved. Obviously every article had its assigned place. Everywhere—on the wall, in the cupboard, on the chest of drawers—there were cartons of wooden boxes with possessions neatly arranged inside. Most of them had their contents inscribed. A keyboard with a variety of keys hung next to the door, each carrying a tag to show the lock it was for.

The youngest child caught our attention. His face was feverish and puffy and swollen around the nose. He breathed heavily with his mouth open. The mother explained: "He always has a cold. He ought to have his tonsils and adenoids out, but we can't afford the trip to the hospital. He would have to be brought back as well, and that means two trips. Perhaps when spring comes." We learned that another one of the children had spent a long time in a Viennese hospital with pleurisy and had only recently returned home, loaded with presents from the doctors and nurses. The girl had come back with a complete set of clothes, some of which by now had been passed on to her youngest sister. Another child was having three midday meals a week at a neighbor's house.

The father told us that things had been going terribly badly these last few days. All they had been able to buy was bread, and not enough of that. The children kept coming into the kitchen asking for another piece; they were always hungry. His wife sat in the kitchen crying. So he decided to go to see the village clerk, who gave him a bag of flour left over from the *Winter Help Drive.* He also received an advance of three schillings on his next payment of unemployment relief. Otherwise they would not have had a mouthful to eat that Sunday.

But how things will continue, we cannot foresee, even assuming that no unexpected changes occur in the external situation. Two developments are possible. As conditions deteriorate, forces may emerge in the community ushering in totally new events, such as revolt or migration. It is, however, also possible that the feeling of solidarity that binds the people of Marienthal together in the face of adversity will one day dissolve, leaving each individual to scramble after his own salvation.

Events of the first type are entirely out of our range of prediction. But as to the second, we can make some contri-

Fading Resilience

89

bution to a question that could become important. How does an individual's life history affect his powers of resistance during unemployment? What connection is there between past experience and present attitude?

Working from sixty-two detailed life histories, we have made comparisons between behavior in earlier times and behavior during unemployment, and we shall summarize our findings here.

We begin with the life histories of a married couple whose present attitude we would characterize as resigned. Their household is running smoothly, and the wife is quiet and pleasant, a good mother who takes pride in her housekeeping. The husband has reduced his standard of living to a considerable extent. He does not go to the tavern any longer; occasionally he goes to the Workmen's Club. He has no plans for the future, but still keeps looking around for work.[3]

J. T., the husband, was born in 1876 in Moravia, one of ten children of whom only he and his brother are still alive. He spent eight years at the school in Grammat-Neusiedl, where his favorite subject was drawing. He wanted to become a carpenter but could not get a job, so he had to go into the weaving mill, where he stayed for three years. Weaving, however, did not interest him, and he went to Mitterndorf. In 1894 the factory burned down and for four months he was engaged in its rebuilding, laying concrete. At that time his brother had already emigrated. He was envious and wanted to be off too. The opportunity arrived when a carpenter who was about to emigrate offered to take him with him, but he decided he could not leave his mother alone. So he never did get away and still envies his brother's experience abroad.

He then came to Marienthal, helped to build the engine house and worked his way up from there to become first a helper in the spinning mill and then an assistant in the machine maintenance department. As a young man he liked to go out a

---

3. These life histories are reproduced for the most part verbatim as they were taken down in shorthand. In general we let the subjects talk, inserting only occasional queries when lengthy time periods were skipped over, and not asking questions until the end.

90   *Marienthal*

lot; there was a group of ten or twelve fellows who would go out together and have fun. He never read anything other than newspapers, and was not interested in sport. From 1914 to 1916 he worked in the engine shop; when the mill closed down he worked in the cannery in nearby Bruck. When they saw that he was the only man in the factory who knew anything about machines, he was given the good post of chief mechanic. In 1919 he was out of work for a short time, then found a job in the sugar refinery. Four months later he went to Mitterndorf to work in the warehouse that belonged to the timber yard; after a few weeks, when his interest in machinery was noticed, he was moved to the central heating unit.

There he stayed four months and then returned to the Marienthal factory, where he worked on the turbines until 1920. When the spinning mill started up he worked there as a mechanic until 1928. Machines had always been his chief interest. He was very proud that this knowledge, which he had picked up all by himself, without any books, had always got him better jobs.

In 1900 he married, just before the birth of his first child. He had known his wife for four years after meeting her at a dance; it had been a very good marriage. Now he had four children, aged twenty-eight, twenty-six, seventeen, and fourteen. The fourteen year old is to learn whatever he likes; the main thing is to learn something. Last year his mother took him to a shop in Vienna and the manager then and there wanted to take him on as an apprentice. She had to promise to send the boy back as soon as he finished school. The father hoped something would come of it. He himself, since unemployment started, had had three months work at the river regulation project, four months building the school, and five months in Mannersdorf. He still kept riding about on his bicycle looking for work. He had no plans for the future; that was something for the younger generation.

He earned some extra money disinfecting premises contaminated by infectious diseases. In the past he used to pay frequent visits to the tavern; he was earning good money then, but now he could not afford it any longer. Most of his free time is now spent at home, in the vegetable garden or looking after the rabbits; now and then he goes to the Workmen's Club. The happiest time of his life were the years before his marriage; he

Fading Resilience 91

didn't have a care in the world then, just had to pay for his keep and could spend the rest of his money the way he wanted. The worst time is the present because there is no money around. Things had been bad during the war too; there had been money enough but nothing to eat. Now it is worse, because the food is here and he cannot buy it.

F. T., the wife, was born in 1883 in Moravia, one of nine children. She came to Marienthal at the age of seven. Her father had been an unskilled laborer. She went to school until she was fourteen; an outstanding student, she would have liked to learn sewing but was unable to as she had to go straight to work in the factory. She stayed until 1912 when she had to leave because her lungs were affected, and has never been back to work since. She married when she was eighteen. Her husband had been married to her sister who died in childbirth after a year. They were married soon thereafter. He was ten years older than she; they always got on very well together and never quarreled. He gave her all his money, didn't drink or gamble and was helpful.

They had seven children, of whom four were still alive. Two had died young, the third at the age of nine because the doctor had given him the wrong treatment. Things are much more difficult now that her husband is out of work. It is hard to make the money last and she has to make nearly all their clothes, even the elder boys'. She needs sixty schillings for two weeks for food and coal, and then there is the milk and meat on Sundays. If any money is left, it goes to the cobbler. During the summer, the eldest son, a painter and decorator, is helping out. Then she can occasionally buy something, such as a pair of shoes or new trousers. She had never bought anything on installments; that was one worry she wasn't going to have.

Her happiest time had been the first years of her marriage, until about 1912. Their earnings had been highest in those days. Then she had fallen ill and had to take care of herself. The worst time had been the war years; there was no money and nothing but *ersatz* (substitute) food. She was worried about one of the boys: he had only ten weeks to go to qualify as a hairdresser when he started having fits of some sort and had been sent home. She would be happy if she could find some apprenticeship for him so that he could get qualified. As a girl she had liked dancing but now she is too old for that sort of thing. She

92   *Marienthal*

still enjoys going to the movie or the theater when there is anything on.

Some measure of resignation or lack of initiative can be
found in the husband's earlier life; for example, he always
wanted to go abroad but had never done so. He still envies
his brother for having realized that ambition. Also, his lack
of interest in reading and sports is a symptom of his resigned attitude to life.

His sickly wife, too, who already as a very young girl put
up with renouncing the career she most wanted, early revealed traits of resignation. Perhaps her marriage to her late
sister's husband also betrayed a limited degree of self-asser-
tiveness. Her former life, like her present, was characterized by a restricted range and a certain easily satisfied
contentment.

This basic attitude continued largely unchanged. What
was formerly a quiet, unpretentious, simple life remained
the same during unemployment, on a reduced level.

An entirely different case is presented in the life history
of a thirty-four year old unemployed man who was now reduced to complete despair.

F. W. was born in 1897 in Marienthal. His father was a brick-
layer. The son went to school from the age of six to fourteen. He
was a rather mischievous lad and had no favorite subject, but
he got on well with the teacher because he respected him. At
fourteen, he entered the factory to learn his trade in the print
works and stayed there two years. Then his father moved to
Neufeld because of a quarrel with his colleagues in the shop.
He was to be bumped by a worker, many years his junior, and
was too proud to take the demotion. Nobody thought of asking
him to stay on in his job, although he would have liked to very
much.

In Neufeld, the whole family again went to work in the factory; in the beginning F. W. did unskilled labor, then rose to be
a machine operator, not paid any longer by the hour but by the
week. He was very happy, fitted in very well, and gave up his
free time to catch up on his education. In 1915 he was drafted.
He could have gotten an exemption but turned it down and

Fading Resilience

93

went. He regretted it after a few weeks. First he went to Vienna for training and then to the Italian front, where he caught malaria which he never got rid of; he is still somewhat an invalid. In 1917 he was put into a hospital and stayed there until the collapse of the Empire.

Then he returned to Neufeld for two years. His parents supported him, refusing to let him go back to the factory because he was too weak; his elder brother had been killed in the war. From 1920 to 1925 he worked on a construction job in Zwillingsdorf. When the job was finished, he returned to Marienthal, doing some unskilled work in the factory. He soon managed to get an office job in the print works. He was very satisfied with it, except that it did not pay much.

In 1922 he married. His wife, who was a year older, came from Ebenfurth. They have two sons, aged two and seven. The whole family is undernourished. Even during the war things were better than they are now. His aim had always been to work his way up, wherever he started. He always put all his efforts behind his work and could turn his hand to anything. If he was given the chance to start, he was sure to work his way up. He is the man who during the first year of unemployment, sent off 130 applications for jobs without receiving a single answer. He has not yet earned a single groschen to supplement his unemployment relief.

Now all hope is gone. He wishes so very much to live by his own earning. His wife, who had never been out to work, is now a complete wreck, especially her nerves; she is always ill and moody. He has no hope left and just lives from one day to the next without knowing why. The will to resist is lost.

In the factory he got his hand in at the difficult office work and was doing well. Even as a young man he wanted to go into a cotton print works. He had been happy there. He would very much like to go to Vienna, if only so that the children could learn something. He would like to let his eldest boy study; if his own plans for a better education had fallen through, at least his children were to have it better but it is not possible.

This man had always made particularly high demands on life. He has been ambitious and hard working, always eager to work his way up. Even his free time was spent on educating himself and—this was decisive—his ambitions were al-

94   *Marienthal*

ways realized, despite his physical debility. The way in which he transferred his plans for his own life to his children was characteristic.

Then unemployment came. At first he still had enough confidence in his own ability to hope that he would find employment elsewhere. When all his applications remained unanswered, he began to grasp the hopelessness of his situation: there was no more room for his ambition, his desire to assert himself and find acknowledgement. This crushing setback broke his self-confidence. The collapse was complete; he even stopped looking for work. His wife, ill and highstrung, runs the household impeccably. At our visit, we were struck by the contrast between his desperate mood and his pleasant, comfortable home. We were told that he used to be an active official in the Christian Socialist Party: now he has given that up too.

We found in our files a number of similar cases, people whose power of resistance, after gradually deteriorating, suffered a sudden collapse. This usually occurred with men whose earlier life had been characterized by ambition and high expectations.

However, those who had been particularly well-off in the past were apt to develop a different reaction to unemployment, as in the following example:

Frau J. K. was born in 1890 in Erlach near Pitten. Her father had been an active member of the Social Democratic Party and consequently had been forced to continually change his place of work. Before reaching the age of six she lived in six different places. The family moving ended in Marienthal, where the political circumstances were quite favorable. The father worked here as a weaver. She was one of five children, enjoyed school very much and learned well without having any preference for a particular subject. She wanted to become a dressmaker, but the other children were still small and she could not leave. She entered the factory as a messenger girl and worked there until 1914. She liked to go out, was passionately fond of dancing, and frequently went to the theater or the movies in Vienna.

Fading Resilience

95

She married in 1910; her husband also worked in the factory. It was a very good marriage; she never had a moment's unhappiness. After her second child she stayed at home and thought she would devote herself to her children. When the war came, her husband enlisted; in 1917 he was killed. At that point the children were one and a half, three, and seven years old. She had to go back to earning a living and began in the cannery. Then she worked for a time for the railway in Mitterndorf, returned to Marienthal in 1920 and worked there until 1929. She now draws thirty-nine schillings relief money.

All her sons have made good. The oldest is a gardener in Marchegg, earning forty-four schillings a week. But he is not giving her anything; he is saving up for a motor bike. The second son works in Vienna, earns forty schillings a week, has part of his clothing provided by the firm he works for, and he sends her thirty schillings a week. She still has to support the youngest boy, who is apprenticed in Vienna. She always made all the children's clothes. The youngest was musical; she let him have music lessons, and even when things were at their worst, she paid seven schillings a month for a music teacher.

She has never lost her cheerfulness and, although "an old girl" by now, still likes to dance. After the war she began to take an active part in the Social Democratic movement, first working in its Women's Section and later in its Child Welfare organization, where she is on the committee. Since the committee had to let the theater go, she now runs the nursery school one afternoon a week. Her hardest time had been between 1916 and 1918, and then last year up to August. During the war things had been bad because her husband had been killed and she was left alone with three children. The situation did not improve until 1918 when, working in the cannery, she was able to get food more easily. Last year had been bad because she had been completely dependent on her sons. She had not been starving, but didn't like depriving the boys.

Her best time was the present because she could see that her children had got somewhere. They all were devoted to her, took her to the movies in Vienna, and looked after her generally. She divides her money so that what she receives from her son, together with the unemployment relief, is spent on food; her pension of fifty schillings a month goes on clothes. When no clothes

96   *Marienthal*

are needed, one eats a little better. She is already buying things
for the boys without their knowing it. She likes to think that
when one of them gets married he will have something put by.

This woman had always shown a great capacity for organizing her life successfully. This ability did not get lost. In
her youth she liked to amuse herself, sought the company
of others, went dancing, and often made trips to the theater.
Today, she still lets her children take her to the movies once
in a while. Work on the Child Welfare Committee, an activity more in keeping with her years, has taken the place of
dancing. Her need for contact with other people has remained the same, and she still knows how to satisfy it. One
has the impression that she has retained her supply of physical and spiritual energy from her better days, from the time
when she used to be at work; her attitude to life is not easily
shaken. To be sure, one cannot say what will happen if her
relief money is cut or her sons lose their jobs.

On the whole, those who had been particularly well-off
in the past either held out for an especially long time or
broke down especially quickly. For those who held out especially long, it was hard to determine how much was due
to economic advantage and how much to adaptability, since
both factors were almost always jointly operative, and had
been there before the onset of unemployment. One woman,
for example, declared that she had no trouble with clothes
because she had been so well provided with them when she
was married; today, ten years later, she is still well
equipped. And she proudly informed us that she never had
to go out to work. In this group of successful people was a
man who in the past had led a very unsettled and adventurous life, supporting himself in first one place then another without ever really being in a bad way, even though
at times not too well off. He treats his present fate as just
another of those adventures which he has always managed
to cope with in one way or another. These people seem to
have both economic and spiritual resources to fall back on.

Fading Resilience 97

On the other hand, the people who had been well off in the past but now put up particularly poor resistance are above all characterized by their complete lack of adaptability. Their life broke because they could neither grasp nor bear the enormous difference between past and present. Some of them give the impression that, because of some early developed mental posture, the original shock effect lasted a particularly long time. Eventually the shock will recede and give way to resignation. With others, however, the feeling of being the victims of an unexpected and undeserved catastrophe is so strong that they show not the faintest sign of coming to terms with their predicament. They seem to be heading for individual disaster long before the village as a whole reaches that point. It may well be that this is the psychological condition which, in a large city, culminates in suicide or a similar catastrophic reaction.

People who had been particularly bad off in the past, now either belong again to the broken families or, consoled by the fact that everyone is in the same miserable plight, have joined the class of the resigned. There is, for instance, the man who years ago was sent to prison because of various illegal dealings while holding a public office. Since then he has lost almost all contact with the other inhabitants of the village. He and his family live in relative isolation and extreme poverty. As a result of his run-in with the law, the family was already in a bad way economically before the factory was closed. In this and similar cases there is no reason for a change in the general attitude to life. The same is true for the family in which the father, an alcoholic, is maltreating and beating his wife and children. For this family, too, the situation has not been essentially altered by unemployment, and consequently their attitude has not changed either.

In some cases, however, where extreme poverty formerly prevailed and (judging from the father's life-history) the family always belonged to the broken group, unemployment brought a certain relaxation. For example, there is the

98   *Marienthal*

mother of three children who lost her husband soon after they were married. Since early youth she has been comparing her own life with that of others in her age group and now clearly finds this comparison less unfavorable. The double burden of household and factory has been lifted from her; she draws relief money, but most important, now her life is much like that of any other woman in the village. Our files contain a number of such cases.

Finally, there are those who in the past led normal working lives with no particular distinguishing features; they are to be found in all three attitude categories. Just which one depends in each case on such factors as age, income, and character traits, but our rough analysis of the past was not sufficient to disclose such differentiating constellations.

Thus we have endeavored, here at the end, to put before the reader a living picture of some of these people with whom we have had such close contact for a few months. This brings us to the limit of our inquiry and also of our method, aimed as it is at the general and typical. We entered Marienthal as scientists; we leave it with only one desire: that the tragic opportunity for such an inquiry may not recur in our time.

AFTERWORD

Toward a History
of Sociography

*The following essay was written almost forty years
ago in an effort to trace the spiritual and methodological ancestors of* Marienthal, *so that our study
could be seen in historical context.*

*At the time, it was the first effort to write such an
historical sketch, attempting to survey the development of three centuries. Like* Marienthal *itself, it
would look different if it were written today, and
there was some temptation to revise it. On reflection,
we decided to let it stand in its original form. Thus,
aside from some minor corrections, we have merely
added a few footnotes (in brackets) indicating where,
in retrospect, we might have added developments had
we seen them as we see them now—forty years
later.*

H. Z.

Throughout antiquity and the Middle Ages there was
little need to survey the social structure of the community.
It was clearly visible to all; everybody's position was traditionally and permanently defined, and whoever overstepped
his borderlines violated public law. Only foreign tribes be-

99

100   *Afterword*

came the occasional object of systematic inquiry. It was the decline of the medieval order that destroyed the simple structure of society. The new entrepreneurs and the free laborers were not part of the old hierarchy; the stability of the feudal order gave way to the uncertainty of bourgeois freedom, and with this change the clear visibility of the social structure began to decline. To regain the view became the task of the variously emerging social sciences—of economics, statistics, and, closely related to them, of sociography.[1]

A New Order

Almost the very day on which the European feudal order suffered its first political defeat became the birthday of the first sociographic study. In 1641, after Cromwell's victory over the rebels, Irish soil was to be settled by the victorious English army. A commission was appointed to report on the economic and social structure of Ireland to gain knowledge that was to assist in the development of the settlement plans. Director of the inquiry was William Petty, later Sir William, distinguished member of the Royal Society, physician, inventor, and in between, founder of the science of political economy, of statistics, and, as author of the so-called *Down Surveys,* of sociography as well.

This great pupil of the philosophical empiricists produced a sociographic study remarkable on many accounts, *The Political Anatomy of Ireland.*[2] The work contains data on the nature and extent of arable land, the methods of cultivation, currency, trade, people, clothes, and food. The report is impressive in its use of quantitative methods, which occasionally lead to points not taken up again until much later. When Petty, for instance, reported that the Irish peasant spent two-thirds of his food budget on tobacco, he was showing an early awareness of the sociographic significance

---

[1. The word "sociography" came much later. The Dutchman Steinmetz was the first to use it.]

2. London 1691; reprinted in *The Economic Writings of Sir William Petty,* edited by Charles H. Hall (New York, 1963).

Toward a History of Sociography

of consumption ratios. Perhaps the most remarkable aspect of this survey was its pronounced insight into the potential role of sociographic investigations. In his preface Petty cited a passage from Bacon's *Advancement of Learning*, referring to human and social anatomy and the art of keeping both the human and the social body healthy. The pursuit of policies without knowing the anotomy of society he likened to the application of old women's quack remedies.

Thus, the first systematic sociographic inquiry began in connection with a problem of social reorganization, in this instance, the colonization of a conquered land. And since this investigation took place in an age of unparalleled intellectual ferment, it marked a first step that anticipated a good many of the later ones.

The social science studies that were to appear in England in the decades after the Civil War dealt only occasionally with sociographic questions in the narrower sense. They were predominantly concerned with problems of economic policy and theory. Not before the second half of the eighteenth century was the development taken up again when the difficulties of English agriculture became a matter of public concern. At that time, the British farmer and farm laborer became the subject of several sociographic investigations.

The writings of Arthur Young,[3] to be sure, are more socioeconomic travelogues than systematic inquiries, but they contain a wealth of new types of observations down to precise details of household expenditures. Young's work was further developed in an investigation into the conditions of agricultural labor conducted by David Davies, Rector of Barkham; his was the first systematic inquiry into the budget of the working classes.[4] Moreover, it was the occasion

---

3. *The farmer's letters to the people of England* (1768); *The farmer's tour through the east of England* (1771); *An inquiry into the state of the public mind amongst the lower classes* (1798).

4. *The case of laborers in husbandry . . . with an appendix; containing a collection of accounts, shewing the earnings and expences of labouring families, in different parts of the kingdom* (1795).

102   *Afterword*

on which that important instrument of modern sociography, the questionnaire, made its first appearance. In 1787 Davies drew up several budgets and sent them to suitable people as a pattern to work from, with a request to report similar budgets from their vicinity. Following Davies' questionnaires, Arthur Young then recorded the household budgets of six families.[5] Sir Frederic Morton Eden's investigation into the state of the poor marked another step forward in survey methodology.[6] Apart from his own observations, he made use of what we today call an interviewer—in Eden's own words, "a remarkably faithful and intelligent person who had spent more than a year traveling from place to place, for the express purpose of obtaining exact information . . . to a set of Queries with which I furnished him."

About that time, when the rapid increase in the number of the poor became a major concern, the first regular reports of private charitable organizations began to appear.[7] Keeping pace with growing industrialization, these reports shifted the emphasis from the agricultural workers to the emerging urban proletariat.

To be sure, these studies amounted at first to no more than well-written observations of a good reporter. Survey methods first achieved real distinction in the famous investigations of the British Parliament, which early established the practice of requesting reports from special commissions to provide data for legislation. The period of reconstruction after the Napoleonic wars and the subsequent era of factory legislation saw a large number of such inquiries,[8] to which

---

5. *General View of the Agriculture of the County of Suffolk* (1797).

6. *The state of the poor: or, An history of the labouring classes in England* (1797).

7. Cf., e.g., *The Reports of the Society for Bettering the Conditions and Increasing the Comforts of the Poor* (1798).

8. The most important of these Reports to Parliament were: *On Conditions in the Factories* (1833); *On the Irish Poor in Britain* (1835); *On Health Conditions in the Towns* (1840); *On Children's Employment* (1863–67); *On the Truck System* (1870–72); *On the Sweating System* (1880–90); and the major *Report on Labour* (1893–97).

Toward a History of Sociography 103

were added after 1835 the semi-annual reports of the factory inspectors.

The techniques employed in these inquiries were varied and often unusually bold. In the Royal Commissions—as distinguished from the Parliamentary Committees appointed in less important cases—representatives of interested parties were joined by experts and by members of Parliament. Then, as to this day, witnesses and informants were heard, cross-examined and, if necessary, confronted with contradicting testimony. The peculiar power of these inquiries derived from the wide publicity they received. Daily reports of the proceedings in the press gave them unusual visibility. The hearings themselves were supplemented by meetings, reports from doctors and inspectors, questionnaires, and, above all, by frequent investigations carried out on location either by the Commission itself or its representatives. The magnitude of some of these investigations is suggested by a few figures concerning one of the later reports, that of the Commission *On Labour* (1893–1897). That Commission met 182 times over a period of several years; altogether 583 witnesses were interviewed, 97,336 questions were asked; 5,350 questionnaires were distributed, of which 2,100 were returned.

The wide-ranging and flexible methods of these surveys made it possible to formulate the problems raised in comprehensive fashion. Investigations into the way of life of some strata of the population were no longer limited to simple descriptions of their economic condition, but gave also views of their moral and intellectual state. The range of sociographically relevant data was thus radically expanded. One need only recall the haunting conversations of children with an investigator, quoted in the report on the employment of children.

Jeremiah Haynes, aged 12: "Four times four is 8, 4 fours are 16. A King is him that has all the money and gold belong to. We have a King (told it is a Queen), they call her the Princess Alexandra. A Princess is a Man."—William Turner age 12: "Don't live in England. Think it *is* a country, but didn't know

104   *Afterword*

before."—Edward Taylor age 15: "Do not know of London."
Henry Matthewman, age 17: "The devil is a good person. I
don't know where he lives. Christ was a wicked man."[9]

Such interviewing went far in anticipating modern test
methods.

Material from some of these inquiries, together with personal observations and newspaper reports, etc., formed the
core of Friedrich Engels' *The Condition of the Working
Classes in England.*[10] The importance of this work does not
lie in the originality of its data but in the context in which
Engels used his material. He attempted to organize sociographic facts in a theoretical framework, in this case the
theory of the class struggle. Here lay the originality of
Engels' work, whose political effect was to prove unusually
great.[11]

Between 1886 and 1900 two additional distinguished and
private social surveys appeared: the eight volumes of *Life
and Labour of the People in London* by Charles Booth,[12]
and a less extensive inquiry along the same lines by B. Seebohm
Rowntree of the city of York, *Poverty, A Study in Town
Life.*[13] In the London survey a large staff of school inspectors, welfare officials and volunteers set out to determine
the standard of living of the poor by means of door-to-door
visits, questionnaires, and an analysis of available census
data. By dividing the population into socio-economic strata,
beginning at the bottom with the "very poor," the extent of

---

9. Commission on Children's Employment, 4th Report, 1865, p.
xxxviii (cited by Marx in *Das Kapital,* in a footnote in Ch. X, The
Working Day, [p. 259, edition International Publishers, New York,
1967]).

10. Leipsig, 1845, New York, 1887.

11. The relationship between the selection of data and the appropriate sociological theory (*Sinnzusammenhänge*) was to become one of
Max Weber's methodological concerns.

12. The survey began in 1886 in the East End, the slum quarter of
London, and was published serially from 1889 to 1897.

[13. We mistakenly failed to mention here the first of these great
studies, Henry Mayhew's monumental *London Labour and the London
Poor* (1851).]

Toward a History of Sociography 105

poverty in London was shown with numerical and graphic precision, illustrated by a detailed set of maps and tables.

The York survey is noteworthy among other things for having introduced the notion of secondary poverty in contrast to primary poverty. The latter is simply living below a certain minimum income level; in secondary poverty this level has not yet been objectively reached in financial terms, only subjectively, inasmuch as certain disrupting traits have led to an irrational use of resources, thus producing prematurely the effects of primary poverty.

Rowntree was also co-author of the first systematic sociographic study of unemployment.[14] Between June 7 and 9, 1910, sixty research teams visited every worker's house in York, to obtain data on the employment situation. In the following months, a short life history of every unemployed man and woman was obtained. One of the main goals of the study was to explore the causes of unemployment.

The high level of English sociography was sustained by the innovation of the follow-up survey, a replica of an original investigations some years later that allowed direct comparisons over time. In 1915 the statistician Arthur L. Bowley published a survey of the economic conditions of working-class households in four English towns.[15] Ten years later the follow-up survey appeared.[16] At that time work also began on the replication of the survey Booth had made forty years earlier.[17]

Quantification

Petty's contemporary, John Graunt, had already been able to demonstrate quantitative social laws when he noted

---

14. Benjamin Seebohm Rowntree and Bruno Lasker, *Unemployment, A Social Study* (London, 1911).

15. Arthur L. Bowley, *Livelihood and poverty; a study in the economic conditions of working-class households* (London, 1915).

16. Arthur L. Bowley and Margaret H. Hogg, *Has Poverty Diminished?* (1925).

17. Hubert Llewellyn Smith, director, *The New Survey of London Life and Labour* (London, 1930).

106   *Afterword*

regularities in the mortality rates of the city of London.[18] About a century later in Germany, a Berlin army chaplain named Süssmilch carried out a similar inquiry into the laws of population movements. Population statistics, which was to become the foundation of the emerging life insurance industry, was followed by the discovery of numerical regularities in the realm of crime. But it was only after the spectacular advances of the natural sciences, astronomy, mathematics, and especially of the theory of probability, that the notion of general quantitative social laws was developed, primarily by French scholars: Laplace, Bernouilli, Fourier.

Condorcet was to create the concept of a *"méchanique sociale"* analogous to Laplace's idea of celestial mechanics.[19] Later, the idea of general social laws received its programmatic basis in Comte's positivist sociology, although Comte himself attached little importance to the empirical development of such laws.

It was Adolphe Quételet who made the first large scale and systematic attempt to apply statistics, considerably enriched by the development of the theory of probability, to the whole realm of human behavior. In his *Physique Sociale*[20]—the title reveals Quételet's grand design—he wrote:

It is much the same with moral faculties as it is with physical ones, and they can be measured if one assumes that they are directly proportional to their effects.

And:

It is even possible to say that one man is braver than another. Such a judgment is based on the fact that two individuals have been observed in their actions and assessed accordingly. . . . Let us suppose . . . that every year, almost without fail, one of them

---

18. *Natural and Political observations mentioned in a following index, and made upon the bills of mortality* (London, 1662).

19. Pierre Simon Laplace, *Traité de méchanique céleste* (1798).

20. *Physique Sociale; ou, Essai sur le dévelopment des facultés de l'homme* (1835).

Toward a History of Sociography 107

has been seen to act bravely on 500 occasions and the other on only 300 occasions.[21]

Elsewhere, Quételet discussed the possibility of measuring memory "with reference both to ease of absorption and capacity for retention," of measuring truthfulness, and of measuring "the degree of foresight shown by different age-groups" as revealed by the records of insurance companies and banks.[22]

Quételet began his career as an astronomer and meteorologist. One of his first publications dealt with the theory of probability. Through Quételet's basic formulations and his attempts to measure so-called psychological facts, new dimensions of social phenomena were opened up for sociography. If human behavior could be measured, it meant that it might be possible to discover causes of that behavior if one could find its statistical correlates.[23]

In Quételet's chapter "On Man, His Development and Abilities," the presentation of crime statistics is followed by the famous suggestion that the realm of social phenomena is ruled by powerful laws.

There is one account that is paid with ghastly regularity; that of the prisons, the galleys and the scaffold.

Quételet then goes on to develop more subtle relationships by showing, for instance, how the likelihood of a man becoming a convicted criminal was related to his age, his social background, etc. He also explored possible links between behavior and genetic background, as well as such

---

21. *Loc. cit.,* pp. 141, 143.

22. Quételet suggested a detailed experimental design for establishing such measurements. An effort to tie these trends toward quantification in the sciences to analogous developments in the structure of the economy was made by Otto Bauer in *Das Weltbild des Kapitalismus,* in *Der Lebendige Marxismus* (Jena, 1926).

[23. Perhaps the most serious omission from this historical sketch concerns the French contributions to sociography that began in the mercantilist period with Colbert's 1665 census and persisted until they linked with the developments described here.]

108   *Afterword*

matters as the relationship between age and productivity among authors of the Comédie Française (to discover, he writes, the "laws governing the comic and tragic talent"). Many of these statistical relationships he presented graphically by variously shaded maps of France and Belgium, showing, for instance, parallel distribution of the levels of education and the rates of crime. These maps, the forerunners of the "spot maps" developed much later by American sociologists, have by now become standard devices in social geography. Quételet thus became the founder of a long series of investigations that were to be listed under the heading of moral statistics.

These investigations did not begin by selecting a problem and then finding the data needed for its analysis. Understandably enough, they began with the secondary analysis of data that had become available as by-products of official administrative statistics on such topics as crime, divorce, illegitimacy, school attendance, etc. At first, these data were presented and strung together without particular aim or method, merely with the vague notion of developing some measurements of "moral" behavior. It was Robert Michels who, in his *Morality in Numbers?*[24] pointed to the ambiguities of this sort of statistical discourse.

An Italian, Alfredo Niceforo, made the decisive step of first establishing his objectives and then hunting for the pertinent data to measure them. He set out to develop indices to measure and compare different societies and civilizations. One of the first of his studies was *Italiani del nord e Italiani del sud* (Turin, 1901), an effort to make explicit the cultural contrast between the population of industrialized northern Italy and the poor peasants of the south. His principal methodological work was *La méthode statistique et ses applications aux sciences naturelles, aux sciences sociales et à l'art* (Paris, 1925).

Quételet's perspectives and Niceforo's theory of symptoms mark only the beginning of the art of describing socio-

---

24. *Sittlichkeit in Ziffern?* Kritik der Sozialstatistik (Munich, 1928).

Toward a History of Sociography 109

psychological processes. Their selection of relevant data from the available material, however, was still haphazard and incomplete; the data themselves, since they were mainly by-products of administrative statistics, were still crude and hence unsatisfactory even when used with care.

The Inventory

It was Frédéric Le Play's idea that a life situation cannot be adequately understood from averages and other indices alone, but only from a full knowledge of all the small details that make one life different from the other. He viewed as especially important a detailed inventory of the things in a family's home and a most detailed knowledge of how it spends its money and what use it makes of its purchases. He was a representative of that other France, whose petit bourgeois and peasant world may have been at the center of the great revolution but was not part of the mainstream of French science.

Le Play was born in 1806, the son of a customs officer in a poor fishing village. Although he was to become world famous, he retained an aversion to city life and a preference for the country people from whose ranks he had come. From the age of twenty-three he travelled widely with friends in almost every country on the European continent, occasionally stopping for a time with a French peasant family or a charcoal burner in the Carinthian mountains, carefully recording everything he found there and saw happen.

In 1855 he published the first results of his travels, thirty-six very unusual family monographs, *Les Ouvriers Européens*. They all had a uniform design: first a brief characterization of each family member by age, occupation, and position in the house; then a description of the relations between parents and children; the general moral rules and conditions that guided their life; and finally a most detailed family budget. This budget recorded income, expenditures, production and agricultural yields, even depreciation of fixed assets. The money value of every item was calculated most carefully so that it became possible to produce, for in-

110   *Afterword*

stance, the budget of a Bashkirian family living almost completely in a bare subsistence economy. "The budget is the key that opens all the doors to the life of the family . . . for all the events that go to make the life of a . . . family appear more or less directly as income or expenditure."[25]

These monographs and others published some years later, *Les Ouvriers des Deux Mondes,* were to become also the scientific foundation for Le Play's conservative and authoritarian ideas for social reform. In the preface to *Les Ouvriers Européens* he explained how the July revolution of 1848 had filled him with a desire to help restore social peace, which, as he saw it, could only be based upon the family. To safeguard its threatened existence was his principal concern.

Yet the historical importance of these monographs lay in a different direction than Le Play thought. The impossibility of selecting "typical" families, with which Le Play tried to circumvent the need for statistics, was his first stumbling block. The sociographic importance of budget figures had been recognized before Le Play, and his arrangement of individual budget items was in part clumsy and dogmatic, as when he painstakingly distinguished between types of income in an unending list of legalistic sub-categories.[26] Also the conclusions he drew from his data proved largely false; his conservative aversion to industry, for instance, prompted him to see conditions among independent artisans in too favorable a light.[27]

The extraordinary effect of Le Play's works stems from a different achievement. He was the first to recognize the sociographic significance of detail and of the detailed inventory. Compared with the shadowy figures of official inquiries, Le Play's monographs have the force of life itself. In his painstaking list of the type and number of sleeping accommodations, bedding, crockery, and whatever other

---

25. *Les Ouvriers Européens,* 2nd ed., vol. I, p. 224.
26. *Loc. cit.,* p. 26.
27. Cf. Alfons Reuss, "Frédéric Le Play in seiner Bedeutung für die Entwicklung der sozialwissentschaftlichen Methode" (Jena, 1913).

Toward a History of Sociography

111

household effects he found, or in his entries in the Sunday budget of a Viennese carpenter (such as "raisins for the fruit cake"), he opened dimensions that traditional sociography had paid little attention to.

Also, Le Play's very method of data gathering constituted a major advance. Noting minute events with great exactness, insisting on comprehensive recording of source material, merging the observer unobtrusively into his field of inquiry—these have become basic ingredients of sociography ever since. Yet the work of Le Play's numerous enthusiastic pupils in France became stultified by dogmatic adherence to the uniform "cadre" of the budget and a rigid rejection of other methods, especially statistics.

The amiable Frankfurt sociologist-statistician Gottlieb Schnapper-Arndt was not a personal pupil of Le Play, but he had an important role in continuing Le Play's work. *Nährikele,* the sociographic biography of his wife's seamstress, is one of the most delightful monographic studies in this tradition, combining statistics with lively and significant detail.[28] His main work was *Five Village Communities in the Upper Taunus.* It advanced Le Play's method in several respects, not only by correcting the design of the budget inventory but above all by making the detailed information part of a precise description of the social setting in which it arose.[29]

The decisive continuation of Le Play's work came from a quarter from which he did not expect it, the statisticians. It had been Le Play's desire to replace the "dead rows of figures" of the statistical survey with a living inventory and attention to graphic detail. He himself did not foresee a synthesis of inventory and statistics. It was the German statistician Ernst Engel who demonstrated his famous budget law with Le Play's data and thereby became the

---

28. Schnapper-Arndt, *Vorträge and Aufsätze,* Leo Zeitlin ed. (Tübingen, 1906). See also his *Zur Methodologie sozialer Erhebungen* (Frankfurt, 1888).

29. *Fünf Dorfgemeinden auf dem Hohen Taunus* (Leipsig, 1883). New edition, Vlg. f. Demoskopie, 1963.

112   *Afterword*

first to bridge the gap between statistics and the monographic inventory. In so doing he was to point to the solution of the conflict that had become so curiously embodied in the two representatives of the French mind, the scientist Quételet and Le Play, whose spiritual roots lay firmly in the conservative soil of petit bourgeois and peasant France.

Engel's Law

We shall now take a closer look at the development of budget analysis. In 1853 the first international statistical conference was held with Quételet in the chair. Following a paper by the Belgian Ducpétiaux, a resolution was passed to the effect that in every country funds were to be raised "to investigate the economic budget of the working classes." In each section of every country three families were to be selected from each social stratum (needy, average, well off) to provide a sufficient basis for comparison.[30]

In the aftermath of the conference, Ducpétiaux himself collected a series of budgets from working class families and published them with a connecting text.[31] These budgets yielded general insights into the worker's standard of living but reflected also on the role of such establishments as pawn shops and public houses in their lives. It was at about that time, and quite independently, that Le Play's *Ouvriers Européens* appeared. Engel, working from the budgets contained in these two works, wrote his paper on "Production and its Relation to Consumption in the Kingdom of Saxony," in which he derived his famous budget law: the smaller the total budget of a family, the larger the share of its income spent on food; hence this share itself becomes the simplest index of a family's standard of living.[32] Ernst Laspeyres and Adolf Schwabe continued Engel's investigations by deriving more refined, if less general, budget laws.

---

30. *Compte rendu des travaux de congrès général de statistique à Bruxelles, le 19–22 février 1853* (Brussels, 1853) p. 157.
31. E. Ducpétiaux, *Budgets économiques des classes ouvrières en Belgique* (Brussels, 1855).
32. *Zeitschrift für das Büro des königlichen sächsischen Ministerium des Innern*, Nos. 8 and 9, 22 November 1857.

Toward A History of Sociography   113

But in combining the individual budget items in broad and significant categories of food, clothing, etc., Engel had not exhausted the possibilities of statistical analysis. He himself describes the reanalysis of Le Play's monographs as "a facade of pearls without a thread." He might have added that in the process, the pearls had indeed lost some of their true value, the significant color of detail.

Carroll Wright, the distinguished head of the Bureau of Labor of Massachusetts, was the first to take things a step further. Inspired by Engel's work, he analyzed 357 budgets of working-class families.[33] He enlivened his statistics to an unusual extent by appending to the budget figures short descriptions of these families in the manner of Le Play. In the budget itself, the individual item derived its significance not only from its dollar amount but also from its status value. Hence there are tables on the sort of meals, the number of carpets, and the musical instruments the families owned. This was the first statistical mass survey to adopt Le Play's idea of the significance of the idiosyncratic detail. Thus Engel and Wright, albeit in a specialized and limited field, were the first to achieve a synthesis of inventory and statistics.

Budget analysis itself has recently made great progress, above all as a result of more work done in the United States. New perspectives for sociological analysis have been gained by applying trend and correlation analysis to family budgets, in order to ascertain the influence of such factors as geographical region or age of the family head. Carle Clark Zimmerman, for example, found that expenditures for intellectual and artistic purposes showed considerably greater variations than expenditures for physical appliances.[34] Budget research made further advances when it was related to statistics of nutrition, an extension that became important

---

33. Printed in the *Fifteenth Annual Report of the Bureau of Labor of Massachusetts* (Boston, 1923).

34. "Principles of Expenditure of Farm Incomes," *Proceedings of the American Sociological Society,* vol. 22, p. 219; also "The Family Budgets as a Tool of Sociological Analysis," *Am. Journal of Soc.,* vol. 32 (1928), p. 901.

114   *Afterword*

wherever the standard of living bordered on or sank below subsistence level.[35]

We have described the development of budget statistics in some detail since it has come to occupy an important position in the sociographic tool chest. Budget figures are among the more reliable indices of the mode of living; they are relatively easy to obtain and lend themselves well to comparisons, both over space and time.

Nevertheless, Le Play's view that the budget was the expression of every relevant occurrence within the family has not been sustained. For instance, such essential concerns as the mode of bringing up children do not necessarily find their expression in the budget. Although the budget may provide significant hints as to the intellectual and moral state of a family, in the end it cannot be more than an expression of the material standard of living, and it must be supplemented by other sociographic data if we are to obtain a total picture.

But while the scope of budget analysis has its limits, the union of statistics and the detailed inventory embodied in budgets suggested a general principle of great importance for the progress of sociography. Traditionally, the information available to the sociographer seldom transcended the data generated as by-products of public administration. The next major advance came when the primary search for data went beyond the buget and aimed at the totality of the significant data. That next step evolved from the work done by the *Verein für Sozialpolitik,* and especially from the work of one of its most distinguished members—Max Weber.

The Verein für Sozialpolitik

In Germany, putting aside the considerable output of administrative statistics, sociographic investigations aimed mostly at social issues of the day. One of the first of these was an inquiry into living conditions of farm labor, spon-

---

35. Cf. S. Peller's concise summary of the relevant problems: *Aufgaben und Methodik der Erhebungen über Massenernährung, Zeitschrift fur Ernährung,* vol. I, p. 247 (Leipsig, 1931).

Toward A History of Sociography   115

sored by the Prussian Academy of Political Economy in 1838.[36] The technique of the survey was fairly primitive. Questionnaires were sent to local committees and agricultural associations, and their answers were published as they came in, without analysis and with not much comment. Little wonder, then, that findings such as these emerged: "the abolition of corporal punishment . . . encourages theft," or "one can only expect the situation to improve . . . when the work-shy are made to work by force."[37]

The following decades produced a number of similar social surveys, sponsored by a variety of official and semi-official bodies, until in 1872 the *Verein für Sozialpolitik* was founded. Through its distinguished meetings and publications it became the center of a great deal of survey activity, and above all of the discussion of the many methodological problems this survey work had raised.

Before carrying out large scale surveys of its own, the *Verein*—which had among its members the foremost social scientists and statisticians of the day—commissioned a special report on the state of the art of making surveys in other countries, particularly in England.[38] Even so, it was not until much later that Germany succeeded in approaching the grand scale of the British inquiries. Evidently, British survey methods were not immediately applicable to the German system of administration, nor was the latter prepared to grant access to data with the same freedom and public support which this work enjoyed in Great Britain.

A whole series of surveys subsequently appeared, inspired by the activity of the *Verein* and by a variety of universities, particularly in Berlin under Gustav Schmoller and in Munich under Franz Clemens Brentano. Although they all dealt with current problems, these studies bore the unmistakable stamp of the historical school then dominant in the German academic realm. Statistical data, as a rule by-

---

36. A. V. Lengerke, *Die ländliche Arbeiterfrage* (Berlin, 1849) p. 113.

37. *Loc. cit.*, p. 285.

38. *Schriften des Verein für Sozialpolitik*, vol. 13 (1877).

116 *Afterword*

products from other sources, supplemented by observations and interviews, were hardly ever used for more than description; analysis seldom went beyond simple comparisons. Efforts to establish casual relationships were rare and advanced statistical methods almost absent. The achievement of these inquiries lay, as did that of the entire historical school, in procuring valuable descriptive data on the various segments of the society and its economy.

Until about the beginning of the 1870s, the condition of agricultural laborers and farmers was in the focus of attention. From then on public concern gradually shifted to the industrial workers. Their problems became identified simply as the *Arbeiterfrage* ("worker question"). And it was only much later that the white collar classes attracted the interest of the survey makers.

A new epoch of sociographic work began with the extensive investigations of the *Verein* into the career decisions of workers in the various branches of industry.[39] This work, initiated and directed by Max Weber and his brother Alfred, consisted of a series of monographs on a number of different factories. The data were collected and analyzed by a team of co-workers according to a plan developed by Max Weber himself.[40] The aim of the survey was to ascertain

on the one hand what effect industry has on the personality, professional career and private life of its workers, what physical and psychological qualities it develops in them, and how these qualities manifest themselve in their way of life: and on the other hand, to what extent the qualities of the workers, as they emerged from the ethical, social and cultural background, traditions and individual circumstances of their lives, conditioned industry's own capacity for development, and the direction this development takes.[41]

---

39. Vols. 133–135 of the *Schriften des Verein für Sozialpolitik* (1910).

40. Reprinted in *Gesammelte Anfsätze zur Soziologie und Sozialpolitik* (Tubingen, 1922).

41. Max Weber, *loc. cit.*, p. 1.

Toward A History of Sociography 117

The core data for the study were obtained from the payrolls and personnel records of the factories in question, and from interviews with the workers and the managerial staff. The inquiry turned on an analysis of the workers' performance on their jobs in terms of their age, sex, social background, political interests, and other such characteristics. The most significant innovation of this survey was perhaps that it did *not* aim at describing something as ill-defined as the "condition of the working class," but focused rather on the personality of the worker, and in turn, on specific factors of his environment. The questions were, "What sort of person does modern industry produce by virtue of its peculiar structure? and what sort of occupational (and hence, indirectly, extra-occupational) life does it afford him?"[42] Consequently, from the many available data on the industrial worker only those were selected that had a bearing on the central problem, and these were then related to each other so as to illuminate the core questions.

The notion of selecting "relevant data" was here a very conscious step in the development of sociography. Max Weber put insights to work gained from a methodological debate that culminated in the writings of the two German philosophers Heinrich Rickert and Wilhelm Windelband. To Weber, social research derives its relevance from the specific cultural significance attributed to human behavior; "it is cultural, i.e., value interests that give empirical scientific work its direction."[43]

However, once the problem was defined—and that was

---

42. Max Weber, *loc. cit.,* p. 37.

43. Max Weber "Der Sinn der 'Wertfreiheit' der soziologischen und ökonomischen Wissenschaften," in *Gesammelte Aufsätze zur Wissenschaftslehre* (Tübingen 1922) p. 277. Leopold von Wiese ("Beziehungslehre"), made an independent approach to the selection of problems to be investigated. Furthermore, a whole series of interesting sociographic works appeared under his direction, e.g., *Das Dorf als soziologisches Gebilde* (Munich, 1928). Von Wiese also performed the important task of keeping German sociography in touch with its foreign counterparts by publishing regular reports of the world's sociographic literature in the *Kölner Vierteljahreshefte für Soziologie* of which he was the founder.

118

Afterword

the second decisive feature of these studies—a great effort was made to reach out as far as possible to make the description complete. Every aspect of behavior conceivably affected by industrial employment was of interest; performance and behavior at work, at home, personal relationships, leisure activities, plans and wishes, nothing short of the whole pattern of life and work became the object of inquiry.

The emphasis on subjective, "psychological" factors was entirely in the tradition of German social science in general, with its stress on ethical problems, and of the *Verein für Sozialpolitik* in particular. Adolph Herkner, one of the leading members of the *Verein,* devoted one of his first publications to the problems of "work satisfaction."[44] In the introduction to his essay on the conditions of agricultural workers east of the Elbe, Max Weber himself wrote:

Even here [in a description of the standard of living] it would be inadmissible to leave subjective factors out of account . . . it is not only a question of how much a worker earns, but whether, subjectively, he and his employer are satisfied with the arrangement and, if they are not, in what directions the motives, desires and interests of both parties tend, because the future depends on both the objective and subjective factors.[45]

It is this pronounced interest of German sociography in "subjective" factors that assured success for even as naive a survey as Adolph Levenstein's *The Labor Problem.*[46] This was a collection of findings from 5,040 questionnaires filled out by laborers, concerned predominantly with their attitudes and sentiments, in short with their inner life more than with their behavior. In spite or perhaps because of the often scurrilous questions ("Do you often go into the forest?

---

44. *Die Bedeutung der Arbeitsfreude in Theorie u. Praxis der Volkswirtshaft* (Dresden, 1905).

45. *Schriften des Vereins für Soziolpolitik, vol. 15 (1892),* p. 6.

46. *Die Arbeiterfrage* (Munich, 1912); see the favorable mention of this study in Herkner's great work *Die Arbeiterfrage,* 6th ed., 1916, vol. I, p. 24.

Toward A History of Sociography 119

What do you think of when you are lying in the forest in utter solitude?"), the book, written with deep seriousness, contains a wealth of interesting data on dimensions that had never before been the object of systematic study.[47]

Here we come to a perceptible deficiency of the surveys carried out under the sponsorship of the *Verein für Sozialpolitik*. Whereas the objective data on age, background, wages, and performance were presented and analyzed with thoroughness and precision, statements on attitudes and sentiments were supported with no more than impressions, at best with a few quotations taken out of context. The development of methods for obtaining psychological data equal in precision to payroll information was to come later and from another source.

It was because of this shortcoming that the studies of the *Verein* failed in their main goal, to describe the total life pattern of the modern industrial worker. The totality that Max Weber had seen as an integral part of the research plan was lost in its execution.[48]

[47. In this context we should have mentioned a somewhat later, charming British study that reached out for new psychological dimensions of poverty, best described by the book's elaborate title: *The Equipment of the Workers, An Enquiry by the St. Philips Settlement Education and Economics Research Society (Sheffield), into the Adequacy of the Adult Manual Workers for the Discharge of their Responsibilities as Heads of Households, Producers and Citizens* (London, 1919). The inquiry used what we today would call depth interviews with a small but statistically representative sample of the manual workers of Sheffield. Love of truth, of goodness, and of beauty were among the dimensions the study sought to establish and grade. This excerpt from the instructions to the interviewers is revealing: "*Leisure*. If you can get him on to his favorite hobby, he will answer all your queries under this head. Don't put questions too abruptly or directly. *Let him talk*, and one by one you will get most of the points you want. If you can *see* his garden, put down your opinion of its condition, etc. Make sure of the trustworthiness of his wife's or neighbour's statement that he is 'always at the publichouse,' etc."]

[48. The rising interest in empirical studies of social issues found an unusually strong echo in Hungary. Around the turn of the century a group of inspired intellectuals, of diverse professional interests, but all with liberal and socialist leanings, founded two institutions which among other things encouraged and published a variety of empirical

120   *Afterword*

The American Survey

The United States was settled at an unusually quick pace, and the influx of ever new, unassimilated immigrants presented a maze of social problems. A growing concern over welfare problems during the 1880s, fanned by the lack of appropriate government policies, led to attempts to study these problems by means of large scale sociographic investigations. In due course, a specific American form of sociography developed out of these efforts, a kind of overall picture called "the survey."[49] A relatively restricted field, originally defined in geographical terms and later with reference to special problems, is described by a variety of methods and from many different angles.

Despite this tendency toward obtaining an overall picture, the American survey can be shown to have gone through stages of development similar to those of European sociography. It began with data from administrative statistics, collected in various government departments, but primarily through a very good decennial federal census. These data were put together and meaningfully related to each other. Figures on population, housing conditions, occupation, illness, crime, and election results were welded into the social whole from which they had originally been taken in order to show their interconnections. The first city surveys were essentially restricted to this reintegration of social data. Yet a concern with welfare problems remained very much in evidence. The great Pittsburgh survey of 1908,

---

studies of social problems in need of reform: The Galilei Club and the review *Huszadik Szazad* (The Twentieth Century). Oscar Jasci, Zoltan Ronai, Sigmund Kunfi, Albert Halasi, and Karl Polanyi were among the leading men of that circle, which profoundly affected the intellectual climate of Budapest before World War I. The volumes of their review are filled with sociographic investigations of emigrants returning from the United States, of living conditions of families on relief, of agricultural workers, of the cost of living, of morbidity conditions, and so forth.]

49. The socio-political origin of the American survey is indicated by the fact that the periodical founded by the "Charity Organization Society" in 1898 and devoted to welfare was retitled *Survey*.

Toward A History of Sociography 121

for example, culminated in an important discussion of the high accident rate in the steel mills.[50]

It is characteristic of the first stage of the American survey that in its original form it dealth with socio-psychological problems only insofar as they were reflected in the official administrative statistics, such as those on divorce and crime. The data required for the survey were gathered in the main from statistics already at hand. The special collection of data was a later development. The Springfield survey (1914) marked a step forward in this direction. (In passing, at least, the connection between Anglo-American sociography and ethnography ought to be mentioned; Rivers' work, in particular, was of lasting influence.)

The technique of the survey then moved in a direction in which description was no longer restricted to the integration of already available data. Surveyers developed greater freedom in the selection of relevant data. Observation of the social process shifted from the points of contact with the administrative system to less visible areas. At that stage comprehensive survey methods that included, for instance, biographical materials, came into their own, and the selection of problems ceased to depend on the more or less accidental availability of data. At the same time so-called psychological data began to become part of the description.

One survey that attracted attention far beyond the circle of specialists was *Middletown*,[51] a survey of a small town in Indiana. In one important respect this investigation marked a great advance. By skillful overall description combined with vivid graphic pictures of school and family life, it managed to convey an overall image of what life in Middletown is like. This quality is illustrated, for example, by the observation that there are two centers of family life

---

[50. We overlooked a much earlier and major American achievement, and with it an important link to the British survey tradition: W. E. B. Dubois' magnificent *The Philadelphia Negro* (1899), a work directly inspired by Booth.]

51. Robert S. Lynd and Helen M. Lynd, *Middletown: A Study in Contemporary American Culture* (New York, 1929).

122   *Afterword*

in Middletown: the dining room and the automobile. But in one respect *Middletown* marked perhaps a step backward; the insignificant amount of attention given to social and political problems, emphasized by the very anonymity of the town under investigation, is a flaw. Interestingly enough, illness, crime, and suicide, the symptoms of decay and disintegration that provided the starting point for the old surveys, are scarcely touched upon.

Parallel to the predominant statistical surveys, a second form of survey developed in the United States which came out of university departments of sociology and social psychology and attached at first little importance to quantitative analysis. The emphasis here was on more detailed structuring of the problem to be surveyed. The first example of these works was a monumental survey, *The Polish Peasant in Europe and America,* by W. I. Thomas, the Chicago sociologist, and Florian Znaniecki. It was the first time biographical material was used on a large scale for a sociographic investigation. With the aid of some 15,000 letters and other biographical material, *The Polish Peasant* described the disintegration of the original peasant family under the influence of emigration and the urban economy and culture on the new continent. By tracing the behavior of these Polish immigrants through changing situations, the authors tried to gain sociological insights. One of the ideas that emerged from that study, one that has been particularly fruitful for the progress of psychology, is that behavior is determined by the interaction of individual attitudes. The *Polish Peasant* tried to document this notion with the help of its wealth of biographical data. Similarly, such later Chicago studies as Frederic M. Thrasher's *The Gang* and H. W. Zorbaugh's *The Gold Coast and the Slum*,[52] did not pursue the statistical analysis of their material.

At the same time elsewhere, the quantifying, statistical survey made progress in connection with many new topics. In a study of lumberjacks in the northwest United States,

---

52. Chicago, 1927; Chicago, 1929.

Toward A History of Sociography   123

for instance, one finds a table of conversation topics: pornography 23 per cent, personal experience and work 11 per cent, criticism of existing conditions 8 per cent, etc.[53] Similarly, the following figures were abstracted to give information about the content of newspaper reports and hence, by implication, to indicate shifting public interest in a variety of problems of special importance to Negroes. The number of lines of print expressed as percentage of the total are compared (in per cents) for two years a decade apart:[54]

	1918	1928
Politics	12	3
Culture	4	15
Events of the day (crime, etc.)	57	53
Sport	6	18
Miscellaneous	21	11
	100	100

Ever more sophisticated indices were being developed: of disproportion between the sexes, of criminality, of the price of land, of houses and apartments, and of shifts in population[55]—even an index of the intensity of an individual's involvement in an organization, built up from the functions he held and from the amount of time he devoted to them.[56]

C. C. Zimmerman investigated the attitudes of 345 farmers to agricultural cooperatives and questions of tariff policy.[57] Interviews revealed (among other things) that hostility toward the agricultural co-operative was a function of the farmer's age and income; and that hostility was strongest among the farmers over sixty who had an above

---

53. Robert Marshall, "Contribution to the Life History of the North-Western Lumberjack," *Am. Journ. of Soc.*, Vol. ? (1924).

54. G. E. Simpson, "Negro News in the White Newspapers of Philadelphia," *Proceedings of the Am. Sociol. Soc.*, vol. 25. (1900).

55. Ernest W. Burgess, *The Urban Community*, Chicago, 1926.

56. "Family Life and Rural Organization," *Proc. of the Am. Sociol. Soc.*, vol. 23 (1900), p. 146.

57. "Types of Farmer Attitudes." *Soc. Forces*, vol. 5, p. 591, and "A Report on Research in Rural Sociology at the University of Minnesota," *Proc. of the Am. Sociol. Soc.*, vol. 23 (1929).

124   *Afterword*

average income. Sociologists similarly began to measure a whole new host of attitudes and value positions—partiality, aversions, social distance,[58] dangers of conflict, etc.

Although these efforts at times were extended beyond their capacity, American quantifying sociography has acted as a powerful stimulus to sociography far beyond the borders of the United States.

If one looks at the topics American sociography has studied, three main problem areas emerge: the city, the farmers and their relations to the urban population, and (closely related to problems of the city) questions of immigration and assimilation. To be sure, there is scarcely an area of society whose problems have not been approached in one study or another: the family, the churches, and so forth. The center of American sociography is at present [*1932*] Chicago and it is there particularly that the techniques of the city survey are being developed. The University of Southern California and, for rural sociology, some of the smaller universities in the Middle West are also playing important roles.

The remarkable development of American sociography is perhaps due to a peculiar limitation of the social sciences in the United States. In a country with a short history, with historical work primarily a subject for the ethnologist, sociographers preferred to direct their foremost efforts to the social problems of the day.[59] In the United States, the "social question" in the European sense has never or not yet emerged, and sociographic studies appear mainly in connection with particular, specific problems.[60] Until recently the relatively great geographic and social mobility has kept "class problems" from appearing in anything like their European form. Typically, it is not class differences but their op-

---

58. Cf. L. L. Thurstone's studies, e.g. "Attitudes Can Be Measured," *Am. Jour. of Soc.*, vol. 33 (1928), 529.

59. Compare this with the enormous influence of historicism in Germany.

60. Above all in the more recent city surveys.

Toward A History of Sociography 125

posite, social mobility, that has been the subject of frequent sociographic investigation.[61]

In the extraordinary development of the technique of the American survey, with its clipping bureaus and questionnaires, its interview procedure often standardized down to the last detail, its research clinics and other innovations, all applied with great uniformity, lies a certain danger of stultification. American sociography has not achieved a synthesis between statistics and a full description of concrete observations. In work of impressive conceptualization—for instance, in *The Polish Peasant*—statistics are completely missing; inversely, the statistical surveys are often of a regrettable routine nature.

The task of integration lies still ahead.

---

61. Cf. for example, P. A. Sorokin and C. Zimmerman, *Social Mobility* (New York, 1927).

Index

Adaptability, 96-97
Attitude toward future, 50, 53, 59-63
Basic attitude, 45-56, 87; of apathetic family, 50-51, 54; of despairing family, 51-52, 54, 92-94; and income, 81-82; and life history, 89-98; of resigned family, 45-48, 87; of unbroken family, 49-50, 53
Booth, Charles, 104
Bowley, Arthur L., 105
Brentano, Franz Clemens, 115

Clothing, 32-34, 80-81
Community participation of observers, 5-8
Community solidarity, 44, 88
Condorcet, Marquis de, 106
Consumer unit, defined, 20n

Data: sources, 2, 4-8
Davies, David, 101-102
Denunciation, 43
Diversions, 63-65

Ducpétiaux, E., 112

Eden, Sir Frederic Morton, 102
Emigration, 57
Engel, Ernst, 111-13
Engels, Friedrich, 104

Family income, 19-24
Food budget, 25-33

Graunt, John, 105

Health, 34-35, 82
Herkner, Adolph, 118

Inactivity, 36-39
Irrational spending, 54-55

Laspeyres, Ernst, 112
Le Play, Frédéric, 109-11, 112, 113, 114
Levenstein, Adolph, 118

Marienthal, description of, 11-16
Mass neurosis, 3

Index

Michels, Robert, 108

Newspaper reading, 39-40
Niceford, Alfredo, 108

Occupational identification, 82-83
Organizational membership, 40-42

Personal relationships, 84-86
Petty, William, 100-101
Political participation, 40-41
Psychological consequences of unemployment, 3, 39, 87-98

Questions of this study, 8-9
Quételet, Adolphe, 106-108

Relief payment schedule, 17, 29
Resignation of children and adolescents, 57-63
Rickert, Heinrich, 117
Rowntree, B. Seebohm, 104-105

Schmoller, Gustav, 115
Schnapper-Arndt, Gottlieb, 111
Schwabe, Adolf, 112
Shock effect, 78-79
Süssmilch (Berlin army chaplain), 106

Thomas, W. I., 122
Thrasher, Frederic, 122
Time structure, 66-77

Unemployed community, 2

Weber, Alfred, 116
Weber, Max, 114, 116-19
Windelband, Wilhelm, 117
Wright, Carroll, 113

Young, Arthur, 101, 102

Zimmerman, Carle Clark, 113-14, 123
Zorbaugh, H. W., 122
Znaniecki, Florian, 122

CPSIA information can be obtained
at www.ICGtesting.com
Printed in the USA
FFOW03n1540100815
15876FF